THOSE FORTY DAYS

CHHANDA-MUNI

Published by Chhandayan

ISBN-13: 978-0-9841-3492-2

Dedicated to

Dr. MAGDALENA NAYLOR

My host

Acknowledgement, without whose blessings, wishes, help, support and sacrifice this Chilla would not have been possible:

Dr. Magdalena Naylor, Alexander Naylor, Dr. Thomas Naylor, Sanghamitra Chatterjee, Dibyarka Chatterjee, Swapan Chaudhuri, Shujat Khan, Ramesh Misra, Nagrajrao Havaldar, Rajyasree Ghosh, Barun Kumar Pal, Gautam Chakraborty, Dilip Mukherjee, Amitabha Bose, Kedar Naphade, Kedar Gangopadhyay, Noelina Arciniegas, Ethan D. Fox, Daniel Weiss, Samarth Nagarkar, Tejas Tope, Steve Gorn, Barbara Bash, Aditya Phatak, Aishwarya Phatak, Dr. Tej Phatak, Amod Dandawate, Bodek Janke, Martina Eichner, Wen Dombrowski, Debu Nayak, Annie G. Singh, Bharathi Venkatraman, Gabriel Halberg, Shailendra Mishra, Ganga (Kelly Kerns), Maggie Herskovits, Puchkie, Zorba, Bella.

Cover design by Anne Couture

Photo on the back cover is by Muslim Harji

1st edition, November, 2016

 Chhandayan Publication
4 West 43rd Street, #616
New York, NY 10036.

www.tabla.org / info@tabla.org

CONTENTS

PREFACE

In the Indian system of practicing music, there is a regimen called *Chilla*. It is a vow one takes to practice as long as he or she is awake, except for short breaks to use the restroom, take a small bite or nap. It lasts for forty days. During this period one needs to be isolated in a chamber preferably with no daylight, to suspend the sense of time. As it can be imagined, it is an extremely challenging discipline, both physically and mentally. Therefore, it is recommended to be done, if at all, within the age of thirty. I took that vow as I stepped into the 62nd year of my life, from July 11th through August 19th of 2016, in an isolated private facility in Charlotte, Vermont. This journal is a documentation of my day-to-day experiences during that period.

The instrument I play is called tabla. It is a two-piece Indian drum producing a variety of tones. The high drum is called *Dahina* and the low as *Bayan*. The *Dahina* is tuned to a particular pitch, while the *Bayan* can be modulated to different pitch variations. There are syllables associated with each individual and combined drum notes, forming into words and sentences, which eventually shape up into a highly developed drum-language and repertoire. One needs to sit cross-legged on the floor to play them with fingers and palms of both hands. Some of the compositions played on these drums are set, and some are meant to be improvised on. It demands a very high level of skill as well musical sensibility.

I have been playing these drums since I was two and half years old. So, the main purpose of my doing this *Chilla* was not to improve my skill, but to gain a deeper insight into the music, which might also further mature my philosophical perspective to music and life. So, what I have documented here is merely fragment of a journey that has been on for almost six decades. That makes me old, but only physically. Mentally I feel as fresh, eager and absorbent as ever. Even physically I feel much younger than perhaps I should. Some of my near ones try to remind me about that. To withstand such coercive persuasion, I say to myself "age is a matter of the mind; if you do not mind, it doesn't matter". I don't mind getting old at all. In fact, it is a lot of fun.

While writing this journal I tried to scribble down the experiences as promptly and closely as possible, without interrupting the process. In those moments, I felt as if I was being dictated and was under compulsion to take notes. So, if I am to be credited for anything at all, it would be for my role of a stenographer.

There is something very important I should mention here. I come from a tradition, in which people are recommended and advised not to share their special experiences; particularly those which are of spiritual importance. So, it was a bit odd to me when I first came across Paramhansa Yoganada's book "Autobiography of a Yogi". It was difficult for me to accept the idea behind a Yogi writing his autobiography. Yogis don't do that, they usually don't have time or interest in such documentation. They would rather spend those times in meditation towards their own enlightenment. Besides, what purpose would it serve? Seekers will find their way on their own. And for the rest, even reading an autobiography of a Yogi wouldn't cause much of a difference. But, when I started looking around and saw the impact it had on the western world, how it influenced and illuminated millions of people all over the world, I became once again convinced about the great value of sharing. It also prompted me to go back in time and realize that all scriptures of the world also fall under the same category of documentation. The fate and state of mankind would have been so different without having them. These realizations removed all hesitations from my mind and I decided to keep this journal for anyone who might take interest.

I have a habit of sometimes bringing in analogies and anecdotes to elaborate a point. Quite a few of such instances may be found in this journal. Please excuse me if they appear as digressions, and give them a chance.

This is the first time I am using the pseudonym Chhanda-Muni, a name given to me by a fellow musician Ms. Rajyasree Ghosh. It means a sage in pursuit of rhythm. A few years back she was staying with us in our house in Nutley, New Jersey. One morning she called me with that name out of spontaneity. I honored and cherished it, but didn't consider myself worthy of it. People see several things in us, we don't. Today I feel a little less awkward with that name. So, I grab this opportunity to honor her feelings, before I hesitate again.

It would be futile to assess this *Chilla* as a success or failure. I don't know yet, and perhaps I shall never know. This is one of those few areas of life which continues to grow its effect on us. Human standards of measurement in terms of success and failure don't quite apply. So, it is better not to worry about those.

Samir Chatterjee

(Chhanda-Muni)

Prologue: Why

There are several historical and theological references to the number forty, some numerological explanations too. Yet, my inquisitive mind is not fully satisfied with any of them. Rational commentators also do not sound totally confident about their interpretations of this mystical number. My mind wants to find out the significance of this number forty in terms of days on its own. Or, rather wants to have its own experience of the period of time and create its own interpretation. That is one of the reasons why I took up this vow for forty days. What is there hidden and can unravel in these forty days?

There is yet another uncertain question in my mind. If my sense of time is to be suspended, how will I keep track of the number of days passed? Question after question; perhaps I shall have none at the end of the forty days.

For me the other reason to do this is that I have been talking about this practice regimen at several occasions to my students and workshop attendees. I have also mentioned about it in my books 'A Study of Tabla' and 'Music of India'. But, I have never done it myself. Until age eleven, when I was home, I was a child. My parents had lost a son in accident before my birth. My mother always thought and believed that I came back to her as a gift from her deity *'Adya Ma'* in response to her dedicated prayer. So, apart from detecting my talent and inspiring me to pursue it, nothing was imposed upon me. At age eleven I was sent to the boarding school in Narendrapur run by an organization called Ramakrishna Mission. It is on the suburb of Kolkata. I stayed there for eleven valuable years of my life, until the completion of my undergraduate degree. Living in that institution, I had to follow their daily routine, in which there was no time slot left open for personal pursuit. The teachers, my friends and the *Sanyasi*s or ascetics were always encouraging my special talent and they still remember me for that. But, I had no opportunity and environment to practice for such long duration of time in isolation. May be I did, during the vacations, had I decided to stay on campus. But, my parents expected me home. I also wanted to be home, with my mother and other members of the family. At that point I also didn't expect Tabla to become my profession. I was all into academics.

On graduation, I came back home and started my masters at the University of Calcutta. I had set up myself for a comprehensive experience of life, 'leaving no stone unturned'. I had already started clay-modeling, leather craft, weaving, knitting, carpentry and painting. Now I added singing and the study of languages to them. I also wanted to earn my own expenses through tuition. So, in spite of being home, I was out most of the days. And, I also had to deal with the Calcutta traffic, although I made good use of those times in the bus by reading. So, my days were full.

Transitioning from high school into college, I started having my experiences of love in its depth and expansion at the same time. There were ecstatic moments of romance leading into breathlessness, absoluteness and numbness. Those were indeed very precious. I hope no one has to leave life without having those experiences. My romanticism matured into marriage at the age of twenty four. Before that I got into a job with the national radio of India known as All India Radio, for which I had to be stationed in Cuttack, Orissa – an eight-hour train ride from Calcutta. In Cuttack I had plenty of time, because life was super slow and the radio administration didn't know how to utilize my talent and caliber. All day I was sitting idle, only except for a few days in the year, when they had a recording of classical music. But, from Monday through Friday I had to be in the office from 10 am until 5 pm. If I found a studio vacant, I practiced, because I loved to. But, even then I wasn't sure that I was going to end up becoming a professional musician. I made several attempts to quit that job, and the higher authorities played games to prevent me from doing so. I don't know what they saw in me. Obviously, it has yielded good results, as far as I can see.

After two and half years of semi-exile, I was transferred back to work at the Calcutta station of All India Radio. Somehow, I became popular to many artists and administrators. They were happy to have me back in the city. Once again, I really don't know what they found in me. I was asked to manage most of the day-to-day administrative affairs of the music department, even though my appointment was as a musician. I was touring with Nikhil Banerjee, Ali Ahmed Hussain and several other stalwart and upcoming musicians. Time flew; in the midst of all those stormy days, I held on to my love for practice and it kept on growing within me.

I am a hardworking person with a lot of will and determination. I am rational and emotional at the same time – the way I always wanted to be. My emotions and rationality are on lease. I release and contract them at will. I have been able to do this through years of practice. There are moments when I don't hesitate to let my emotions and impulses take over. Then there are also moments when I invite and engage all aspects of my mind to have a discussion. I allow them the time they need. I am sensitive and careful. I know how to monitor myself. I didn't always need my Gurus, parents or elders for everything. Occasionally, I would go up to them for insight and guidance. But, I have been always aware that there are lots of things in life which I have to figure out by myself. I also know that certain things in life need to be earned. If one is able to envision them and aspire for them, they need to be pursued with a lot of diligence and discipline. Diligence and discipline, for the most part, are genetic. It helps a lot if they are inherited. Much of them can also be acquired from environment or by following influential examples, such as teachers, role models and Gurus. But, to benefit from those surroundings, there needs to be some amount of inner motivation; even a little would help.

The purpose of this austerity for me is not to enhance skill, but to seek insight, which can come only through involvement.

In preparation

It is 12.39 am on July 10th. In two days I shall be entering that room of isolation for forty days, to practice as long as I am awake. The only reasons I might stop would be to use the restroom, take a bite or a short nap. In all of these three excuses, the urges will go through multiple levels of verification before being addressed. There will be no indulgence of any kind. It is called the *Chilla*.

I became familiar with this discipline of practicing music much earlier in my life and always felt fascinated by the concept. But, as I said earlier, I could never manage the time and determination together to actually do it. I have done something similar, practicing continuously for several hours and days. But, it has never been for forty days. When I started developing the urge to do it, my life kept on becoming busier and busier, dedicated to fulfilling the wish of the Supreme. Through advanced planning, which also called for making sacrifices, I was finally able to isolate these forty days from my schedule of activities. Other than time and determination, there was another obstacle - my body. *Chilla* is recommended to be done within the early part of life, not exceeding the age of thirty. It is imaginably extremely demanding on physical and mental abilities. My body has been in use for sixty one years. It is not young and fresh anymore, as required for such austerity. It has its wear and tear, discomforts and pains. In spite of all of those issues, last summer going through the Ayurvedic intense cleansing process called *Pancha-Karma*, I got an affirmation from the treating doctors that my body was younger than it normally is at my age. So, without any further hesitation, I blocked this period of time.

The choice of place happened in a miraculous yet natural way. Initially, I thought of doing it in my new apartment in Sodepur, part of the new extended territories of Kolkata, India. In addition to the isolation, there is also a very dependable support system. But, during the initiation ceremony of Alexander Naylor, Todd Miller, Tripp Dudley and Aditya Phatak on February 13th of this year, which was the day of *Saraswati Puja**, I came to know Alexander's mother Dr. Magdalena Naylor a little better than before. I had met Magdalena twice before. The first meeting was in Dartmouth, New Hampshire with her husband Thomas. At that time Alexander and I were just growing acquaintance.

The second time was in New York City when we went for lunch to a Greek restaurant.

---

* *Saraswati* is the Indian goddess of knowledge, wisdom and all kinds of artistic pursuit, including music. *Puja* is the Indian word for worship. The day of *Saraswati Puja* is considered auspicious for initiation.

This was after Thomas's untimely death. On both occasions I couldn't fail to notice her stand-alone individuality, which could be somewhat embarrassing to her immediate family. She appeared to me as a radiant energy of positivity. During the initiation ceremony in my house in Nutley, NJ I got to see some other aspects of her – her loving, caring and selfless service-oriented mentality. Some of these may be somewhat attributed to her Polish origin. But, she is a tad more than that. When she genuinely invited me to her place saying that her house is practically empty, it occurred to me that this would be an ideal place. What further added to the appropriateness of the venue is the weather in Burlington, Vermont, which will be much more favorable than the weather in Kolkata during these months.

Since May 28th, the first day of this year's three-day long Annual Tabla Ashram*, I have been finally preparing for it - sitting and practicing for long duration of time, keeping hunger waiting beyond the usual wait time and treating sleep more as nap. And, there were some other abstinences too. Observing these for more than a month, I have been feeling increasingly lighter and ready for it. I am hoping the transition will be relatively smooth.

---

* *Ashram* is a Sanskrit word for hermitage. And, the Annual Tabla Ashram is a gathering of musicians to learn and practice tabla in an unbroken spell of time. This year it was held for three days, from 9 am until 9 pm.

Tonight I am staying at the residence of my dear friends Steve Gorn and Barbara Bash in Accord, New York. I came here after a performance at the Maverick festival. Tomorrow morning, or rather later this morning, I shall drive up to Alexander's house in Charlotte, Vermont. I am driving a vehicle rented from Newark, New Jersey airport, which I shall return to Burlington, Vermont airport tomorrow afternoon. My student Tejas Tope drove me to the rental car station in Newark airport. In the past couple of days my wife Sanghamitra, son Dibyarka, disciple Aditya and his mother Aishwarya Phatak helped me in packing for the trip. Another disciple Amod Dandawate came to see me two days before I left. The exchange of our final looks was memorable. I saw a question in his eyes: who is this man, do I know him?

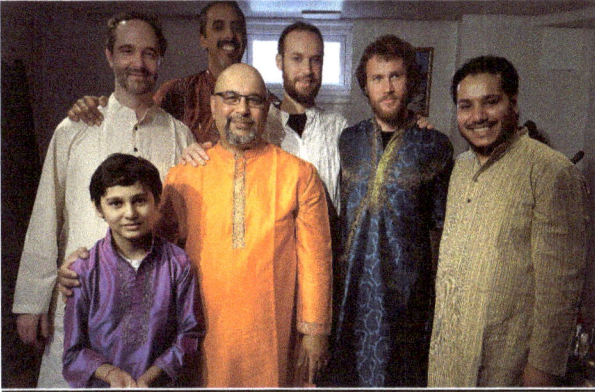

February 13th,2016; (from left)
Front row - Aditya Phatak, Samir Chatterjee,
Back row - Todd Miller, Nano (Emiliano A. Valerio) ,
Tripp Dudley, Alexander Naylor, Dibyarka Chatterjee

Photo credit: Wen Dombrowski

The day started as beautifully as it could, with a lovely fruity breakfast in the company of Steve Gorn and Barbara Bash on their patio. This patio always reminds me of the time when my mother was sitting on it and Steve Gorn shared his observation that "she carries a heaven in her mind wherever she goes". There were other people in the group that day, including my elder sister and my musical colleague Barun Kumar Pal. But, she was noticeably different. This morning none of us had to rush. So, we engaged in conversation. Topics traveled between mysticism, misuse of religion, social and political issues of the USA and the fate of human beings caught in that chaos. Eventually I had to leave and they had to continue with their day. I touched their feet and started my journey.

In a couple of hours the mountains and the landscape of Vermont greeted me. The moving clouds drizzled and poured as I moved deeper into Vermont. To me they signified purification. Xander met me at Burlington airport and transferred all of my stuff to his car before I returned the rented car. We drove home. His mother Magdalena and girlfriend Maggie were eagerly waiting for my arrival. They, along with the two dogs Zorba and Bella, greeted me with all the warmth and exuberance one can ever expect. I am indeed very fortunate. I received all of those with humility and gratitude.

Alexander and Maggie had to drive back to New York. So, the first thing I needed to do was to check the room I shall be in. It was the perfect amount of space and a combination of my favorite colors – purple, sea green, different shades of blue and white. There is a bed, a sofa, three chests, two tables, two bedside stands and a few lamps. The room has four skylight windows. There is a window air-conditioner and a table fan, pretty quiet. There is a room annex to the main room. It has two small tables, four chairs and a large window with a window air-conditioner. This room's ceiling is of normal height. There is beautiful spacious bathroom attached to the annex room. Everything is clean and fragrant.

The Spot and the bed

Photo Credit: Samir Chatterjee

The Skylight

Photo Credit: Samir Chatterjee

Magdalena carried a carpet upstairs to my room and spread over a spot I chose to sit on, facing east. She had carried out the two chairs which were sitting on that spot. Alexander had already brought my set of tabla to the room. I set them up and played a little. It was responding very well. That would be the spot. Magdalena later told me that Alexander always chose that spot to practice. Alexander and

Maggie brought in all of my stuff from the car. My stuff - I always remember George Carlin's amazing episode on 'The Stuff'. It is driven by so many hypothetical 'what-if' factors, that we keep on piling up beyond our capacity to consume, let alone being able to carry. So, what have I brought?

The Stuff

Photo Credit: Samir Chatterjee

The Stand

Photo Credit: Samir Chatterjee

Food:

1) one 24-pack box of energy bars: 12 chocolate chip and 12 crunchy peanut butter,

2) two 18-pack boxes of nuts and spice bars: 9 of dark chocolate, nuts and sea salt and 9 with maple glazed pecan and sea salt (5g sugar),

3) one 35-pack box of chewy granola bars: chocolate, almond, sea salt with chia,
4) one 2 lb. bag of cashew clusters with almonds and pumpkin seeds (50% cashews, gluten free),
5) two bags of 12-pack antioxidant mix of pistachios, almonds, dark chocolate, cranberries, blueberries and raisins,
6) four bars of glazed peanuts and one small bar of black sesame.

Drinks:

1) Nine 1-liter containers of 100% natural coconut water,
2) 35 bottles of Gatorade Fierce,
3) 100 tea bags of Earl Grey,
4) Natural sugar.

Supplements:

Fish oil and Vitamin D3; I have been taking them for some time.

Medication:

Advil and vitamin C, just in case.

Clothing:

Mostly indoor clothing for warm weather, except a woolen vest, a sweater and a shawl.

Accessories:

1) CPAP machine,
2) Laptop with external hard drive. I forgot to bring the charger. Magdalena miraculously brought out a perfect charger from her closet!
3) A CD-cassette player,
4) A flip video camera,
5) A digital audio recorder,
6) Radel Sunadamala, an electronic player of melody lines of *tala*s (rhythmic cycles),
7) Two I-phones with chargers,
8) Batteries,
9) Two pairs of eye glasses,
10) Six notebooks and a pen.

Study materials:

1) Cassettes from lessons with my two Gurus Amalesh Chatterjee and Shyamal Bose,
2) Copies, notebooks and diaries with written compositions from the past.

Alexander had already stacked up a lot of water. Magdalena set up one coffee maker and one tea maker on one of the tables with some tea bags and tea leaves. I am all set in half an hour. The set-up is so perfect that I changed my mind and decided to start from tomorrow.

Before Xander and Maggie left, we chatted a little over a cup of tea. I related to them the recent episode about the split kurta (long shirt). What happened is this:

A few days ago on July 2nd and 3rd I was a joint-convener and performer in a music program held at the Penntop Ballroom of Hotel Pennsylvania in New York City. There were simultaneous programs going on at the Madison Square Garden and Hammerstein auditorium of Manhattan Center. Chhandayan, the not-for-profit organization I am president of, was collaborating with North American Bengali Convention in presenting the classical music programs on those two evenings.

On July 2nd I was only organizing and presenting. But, on the 3rd I was scheduled to play with two maestros – violinist L. Subramaniam and vocalist Ulhas Kashalkar. Both of them usually dress white or off-white. In order to put an accent to the eyes of the audience, I decided to wear an orange kurta. After dressing up, I was on my way out when the left pocket of my kurta got caught up in the door knob and split. I felt a bit sorry and embarrassed for my carelessness, but very quickly changed to another kurta and went out. Before I left, I showed the split pocket to my wife Sanghamitra, wondering if she wanted to give it a shot. She has a special talent in mending. But, for this type of injury, she recommended taking it to the hospital - my tailor in Kolkata.

Three days later, on Wednesday, I was doing a routine scroll down through my personal

Facebook page, just to make sure that there was no junk in there. Suddenly my eyes got stuck on a picture from this year's *Saraswati Puja*, the day when I initiated Alexander, Todd, Tripp and Aditya. They were all there in that picture with me, my son and another disciple Nano. To my utter surprise I see myself wearing that orange kurta, which I was trying to wear on July 3rd. Before wearing a kurta I usually do a final press to even out the crease, if any. On this occasion, I had noticed some crease indicating that the kurta had been previously worn, at least once. As revealed in that Facebook picture, I wore it on that day. For the initiation I try to wear something new, never worn before. So, I chose this kurta because it was new. I realized that the split pocket was clearly an interception from my wearing it for any other purpose.

Going back a few summers, I was invited to accompany Swami Tejomoyananda, who at that time was holding the highest position in the order of Chinmoy Mission, a worldwide spiritual organization. It was to be held at the Raritan Convention Center in New Jersey. Swami ji was scheduled to do his *Bhagavat Katha*, the discourse based on the miraculous deeds of Lord Krishna as described in the *Bhagavat Puraana*. During his discourse, he also sings some *Bhajans*, devotional songs. He is not a 'singer', but is tuneful and has a beautiful voice, rich with emotional quality. Being persuaded by two elderly friends, I agreed. It would go on for a week. Every day, after his discourse, there would be worship and chanting followed by a classical program featuring maestros like Vilayat Khan and Jasraj.

On request from Swami Tejomoyananda, I arrived a little early on the first day. We found a room to tune and practice a little. I knew he would be singing from the key B and I took a tabla set accordingly, almost tuned. Within a few minutes of rehearsal he became satisfied and confident, ready to go on stage. There were about five thousand people attending the convention every day. Half way through the first session of his discourse, Swami ji started feeling connected with me. There was a personal touch of genuineness and freshness in his deliverance, which drew my attention to him. Such mutual connection brought us together. Rest of the week it seemed like it was just the two of us; others were only witness.

On the seventh day as he was wrapping up the discourse, I was waiting for his indication to pack up my drums. He realized that and gave me the signal. I picked up the cover for the *Dahina* (the right-hand tuned drum) and, to my utter shock and surprise, noticed that the *Dahina* was split in the middle. There was no such indication until the last note I had played. On the contrary, the *Dahina* had perfectly settled after a little bit of tuning on the first day, never needing an additional tuning. Every day it continued to open up more and more, almost singing. Swami ji was making announcement about the rest of the proceedings scheduled that evening. When I was able to draw his attention to what just happened and show him the split *Dahina*, he shivered in reaction and spontaneously murmured "It is not the will of the Divine for the *Dahina* to be used for any other purpose". Thousands of people witnessed and heard that.

This happened on a Sunday. On the following Wednesday I received an envelope from Steve Gorn with a postcard in it, a picture of Lord Krishna. He had also included a note saying that he had picked it up during his recent trip to the Vrindavan, the holy city in India associated with Lord Krishna's early life activities, and thought that it should belong to me. It was happening all out of the blue. That weekend I had a Jazz gig. I decided to wear the same off-white raw silk kurta I was wearing through the week of the *Bhagavat Katha*. The kurta was fine, even after being worn for a week. There was no sweat or stain. We were heading out for the concert, all loaded, Sanghamitra is in the car. I came upstairs only to turn the alarm on. After turning it on I was stepping out, and the left pocket of the kurta got caught in the door knob and split. The split on July 3rd this year was identical to its precursor.

I try not to make any immediate conscious effort to connect such incidents and draw inference from them. Yet, they do draw my attention and make me ponder upon. Dr. Magdalena Naylor pointed out this important aspect - that I notice. There is a stand on the north-east corner of my office room in Nutley with the split *Dahina* and the picture of Lord Krishna sent by Steve Gorn.

After Xander and Maggie left, I came to my room to change. At 7 pm I went downstairs for dinner. It was clear daylight. Magdalena took me around her garden, we were walking barefoot. She recently cleaned up a lot of bushes and uncovered an interesting circular rock formation under some tall trees.

We chatted more over the dinner. The topics were quite a few, all very interesting and meaningful. She was open and frank in telling me about her miraculous recovery from the fourth stage of uterus cancer. The doctors were uncertain about the effectiveness of the treatment they were applying on her. They didn't see her responding even after two weeks of radiation. But, from the third week she started responding. Feeling a little better, she left for her projects in the villages of Uganda and came back in a better shape, physically and mentally. During her treatment she made another trip to Tibet, Nepal, Mustang and a few other Asian places and returned with her lungs cured from metastasis. She is a psychiatrist, focused on pain management. To be more specific, she is right now preparing to research on human ability to self-produce morphine in overcoming pain. She has a trip to Uganda from July 15th through the 31st. In Uganda she is working in a project called Imaging the World, launched and carried on by her friend. They help local nurses and midwives to use modern imaging equipment, such as ultra-sonography, and electronically communicate with the centers with better diagnostic facility.

She maintains an extremely active and productive life. So, even when she is here, she will be out of the house quite a bit, attending her intense schedule. She explained to me several things about the house, to cover all emergency possibilities. She also passed on the information about a masseuse she found the other day in Burlington, who could come home for treatment, if needed. Then she fixed my bed and we said good night.

I have taken a picture of myself a few hours ago and my weight right now is 188.4 lb. I brought my shaving kit, except the shaving cream. Dr. Naylor suggested me to take that as an indication that perhaps I am not supposed to shave. She assured that it won't bother her at all, if I bump into her in the house unshaven.

Forty Days

Ma – Jyotsna Chatterjee

Photo Credit: Jack Vertoogen

I woke up with a dream of my mother singing a Tagore song

"Dnaarao aamar aankhiro aage,
tomaro drishti hridaye laage"

25

Please stand in front of me, let your vision touch my soul.

Who or what am I expecting to stand in front of me!! This has been the question of my life. By now I know for sure that there is a presence. I have grown to be convinced about it through several personal experiences, which cannot be all left to coincidence. But, what is it? Do I ever get to have a closer perception? Any sort would satisfy.

It is interesting to observe how my mother appears on such an important moment of my life. The last time she appeared in an early morning dream like this was on the day of my finding the sacred space of Chhandayan in the heart of New York City. In that dream she came to tell me "Don't worry; I am going to help you in realizing your dream. Now that I am free from the confinement of my physical form, it is easier for me to do things for you." This was shortly after her death.

Yes, of course, I was thinking about her yesterday, as I do every day. I was also thinking about so many other people. Yet, she happens to be only one showing up at that perfect moment. Besides, it is a bit unusual for me to dream. I am more of a day-dreamer. This morning she was wearing a white sari with blue border and was standing while singing. Towards the end of her life she used to have difficulty in sitting on the floor. She was accompanying herself on some sort of a wooden keyboard placed on a stand. It looked somewhere in between an upright piano and an organ. As she went through the first couple of lines of the song, the keyboard was just about to fall off the stand. There were people around her, but no one was paying any attention. I yelled from the audience "Ma, wait for me". She froze right there. I woke up.

I don't know what time it was, I don't need to know. I brought a wrist watch, which ran out of battery and stopped working yesterday on my way to Woodstock. After using the restroom, I went straight to the tabla. I started enjoying the freedom of time. I am happy to have the openness of time to work on the materials I always wished to address in such state of freedom. I played pretty much all day. There were moments of heaviness and lightness. I was adjusting to the space. I took a nap later in the morning, which helped. The morning and afternoon spells were longer, more consistent and productive. I started going through my previous notebooks and found a couple of my own compositions which were making a lot of sense even now. So, I isolated them to take a closer and deeper look.

I had a granola bar, a cashew cluster, a small portion of sesame bar and three quarters of Gatorade until the evening. Magdalena brought a lot of food in the evening. I had lentil soup and vegetable pierogis with cheese salad. We chatted about our days and I went back to more practice.

Day 2 : July 12, 2016

It is a very different morning! I am more concentrated, settled and lighter. I played different patterns of 'dhere-dhere', a movement that involves the right-hand palm, on and on in slow, medium and fast tempi. I felt totally present and focused on every touch, every note and every tone, continuously drawing inspiration from being within that process. I was missing this yesterday. I just had breakfast. Hearing me in the kitchen, Magdalena came down and gave me two eggs with tomato on the side and coffee. I also had a small cup of yogurt. She didn't like my diet yesterday and wants me to eat properly.

Coming back to my room I immersed into my practice going deeper and deeper. My hands and fingers were happy, giving me a lot of joy and inspiration. I chose to focus mostly on my own compositions. The strength and mobility in my left hand on the *Bayan* gave me not only a sense of perfection but also a lot of flexibility to move into different directions. Almost everything seemed to be working well. They seemed original. I kept on playing until dark. I didn't get up to turn the lights on.

Towards the end of the practice session a realization gave a chilling sensation through my spine. I realized that I am playing on the same *Dahina* I used at the Raritan Convention Center a few years back during the *Bhagavat Katha*. This *Dahina* originally belonged to my dear friend Anindo Chatterjee, a great tabla maestro. One winter evening, during my visits to Kolkata,

I was sitting in the shop of my tabla-maker Shyamal Das. As he was putting the finishing touch on my tabla, Anindo came in to pick up his *Dahina*. He was returning home from a concert at Rabindra Sadan. We sat next to each other watching Shyamal work on our drums, over cups of tea and sweets. I asked Shyamal to finish Anindo's *Dahina* first, it was almost ready. He put a final touch and handed it over to Anindo. Anindo asked me to check it for him. I played a few strokes and it sounded perfect. Seeing me so satisfied, Anindo offered me the *Dahina*. He invited me to a concert next afternoon at Belur Math, the headquarters of the Ramakrishna Mission order situated on the western side of river Ganges. It was a jubilee celebration of their college and Anindo was playing a concert there with Amjad Ali Khan. He came to pick up this *Dahina* for that concert. He asked me to come to the concert and take the *Dahina* from him after the performance. It was easy for me to go there, only a ferry across the river from my residence. So, I was there and he literally handed over the *Dahina* to me on the stage right after his performance. Incidentally, Swami Chinmoyananda, the founder and main spirit of the Chinmoy Mission, had a connection with the Ramakrishna Mission. He was a close follower of Swami Vivekananda, the founder of the Ramakrishna Mission order and Belur Math.

After the *Dahina* had split, I got it re-headed and tried it a few times. It never sounded that good. So, I moved it to the back row on my shelf of *Dahina*s and gradually forgot about it. This winter when I was going to Kolkata, I had no luggage to carry. So, Dibyarka suggested that I take a few drums worth getting re-headed by Shyamal. This *Dahina* had joined that group and went back to Shyamal. It came back in a shipment in June, while I was touring Germany and Spain. On my return, Dibyarka placed all of my repaired drums by my seat in the practice room. I chose to practice on this one and eventually packed it to use during my *Chilla*. While checking the drums, Dibyarka suggested that this *Dahina* would sound best in B flat. But, now it is tuned to B, where it was almost 10 years ago. It is amazing to observe the concurrence of events and their implications. Even if I try to avoid any biased conclusiveness, it certainly makes me ponder upon the factual connections.

Magdalena came late and made some extraordinary dinner for me with baby spinach salad, steamed salmon, honey mustard sauce, yogurt with dill and rice on the side. I stayed up long after that, but didn't play. Towards the end of the practice session I felt some pain creeping up in my back. I don't want it to spread any further.

Day 3 : July 13th, 2016

There is no aim or accomplishment in this process. The only important thing is to do it – practice for the sake of practice. This understanding was stable in my mind all of yesterday. The day has passed without an opportunity to scribble down a word. The morning was a bit confusing compared to the rest of the day. The level where I ended yesterday was all gone; nowhere to be found. I kept on going and waiting for their return. Instead, I started having a relapse of the back pain from last night. I lied down and fell asleep. At some point I woke up and started having that freedom and lightness back at a much higher level than yesterday. It seems as if the tabla was talking to me as a guide, showing me areas I have never seen before. They emerged out of some compositions and phrases, which I had played a million times before. But, now they are sounding so much more expressive, poignant with sublime qualities. I was amazed! The day passed with a lot of joy and happiness.

It rained before dark; after Sunday this was the first rain.

I was also able to detect the cause of my back pain. It is due to some cold infection I may have picked up. No idea when and how, but it is there. Dr. Naylor gave me a mug of concoction - honey and lemon squeezed in lukewarm water. My nose started running. I hope tomorrow to be an even better day.

Day 4 : July 14, 2016

The mind is much more settled on chosen themes; or it is still settling, I should say. I could practice one single pattern for much longer than earlier. As I go on, the mind does drift away to the thoughts of all the people, living things and objects I have come to know, even the sky. How do you think about the sky, what do you think? The Sky is so different from those mountains or the woods at the distance. Those things or even any form and shape of water are much more comprehendible through our perception than the sky. Even the other elements of nature, such as air or fire, are comprehendible through touch, smell and even taste. We cannot touch the air, it touches us detectably only in motion. Its smell is from what it carries. But, the sky is not only so distant and spread out, the only way we can perceive it is through vision. Yet, that perception could be totally false, an illusion. Is there really something as the sky? Perhaps not, it is just an open space. Yet, it occupies such a huge portion of our experiences in life – in our thoughts and imaginations. Politicians try to create territorial divisions even in the sky. How can you divide something which doesn't exist? What happens to human beings when they become politicians?

But, I was able to rein my mind back to those chosen patterns and compositions with much less effort and much more focus. There were moments when I felt light and happy. There were other moments when it was very heavy and painful. If it started hurting in one phrase or a type of movement, I left it there and went on to something else. But, I kept going.

Day 5 : July 15th, 2016

Today I didn't stop when it hurt. I slowed down and kept working on the same thing for much longer duration. My mind was steady and focused. Any sound other than those from my tabla startled me. I balanced my attention between the left and the right hands. I am taking these measures towards continuity. There was one occasion when the back was hurting too much. I lied down on the carpeted floor for a while and it went away.

Sometimes the fingers were ecstatic, sometimes they won't move at all. Later in the day I was becoming very critical of myself, a little too harsh perhaps. I was whipping myself for my inabilities. This went on for a while. But, then at one point things started changing. The things I thought I could not do were appearing to me out of nowhere. As if you are upset wondering where is everyone in the house. And, then everyone starts appearing out of their rooms greeting with a smile.

Zorba - outside the door, listening and meditating to my *Chilla* practice

Photo Credit: Magdalena Naylor

Very early in the morning Magdalena left for Uganda. The dogs are with her friend Josh. I am missing them, particularly Zorba. Magdalena noticed that when I am playing, Zorba lies on her chest outside my door. But, when I stop playing he sits or stands up. The door is at least 30 feet away from my practice spot. Zorba is named after Zorba in the movie Zorba, the Greek. He is truly different.

Magdalena has stacked up a lot of food and insisted on finishing them before she returns. So, I am eating real food – eggs, fish, chicken, vegetables, fruits, yogurt, salad, etc.

Day 6 : July 16, 2016

It is interesting to notice how certain things tend to move up in speed much quicker than others. My intention is to go up in tempo with all notes and phrases intact, leaving nothing below. But, it doesn't happen that way; it forces me to make a hard choice. The more difficult and heavier phrases, which I would not like to leave behind, are asking me to go ahead. They try to assure me to be there always as my foundational strength. It is a very strange sacrifice they make! From my past experience, I know that no matter how hard I try to climb up with everything, there will always be a gap between the more difficult and the relatively easier materials. It is because the more I work on the harder things, the easy becomes even easier.

I am measuring myself in many different ways – tempo, clarity, articulation, dynamics, linguistic and poetic justification, strength and stamina, etc.

It has been my habit for a long time to call my son Dibyarka or disciple Daniel Weiss or someone equally close when I come across something new and exciting. In the same way calling my wife Sanghamitra, even to hear her voice, has been part of my life for several years.

I am resisting all of those temptations. I am recording some of the new musical ideas and also making these entries in the journal. That is all; nothing beyond in terms of my inclination towards communication.

Twice I noticed tears in my eyes. I don't know if they were tears, some drops caught in the eyes fell off. When and how these happened is not known to me; probably while I was practicing.

Day 7 : July 17th 2016

Those were tears indeed. They appeared again this morning. My mind was tender, full of gratitude as I was working on one single pattern for over an hour.

I had another early morning dream. In that dream I was exploring a few rooms in the backstage area of a concert hall. Roaming around I entered a room, which could be a green room. But, the carpet and all furniture were close to Azure or UN blue, can't tell. There was a huge mirror on one of the walls, and in that mirror I saw a reflection of Amalesh da. I used to refer to my Guru Amalesh Chatterjee as Amalesh da; 'da' is shortened form of *Dada*, meaning elder brother. I met him at the Ramakrishna Mission in Narendrapur and it was customary there to address our teachers as *Dada*. My other Guru Shyamal Bose was also popularly known in the Calcutta music scene as *Barda*, elder brother.

In my dream Amalesh da was wearing a blue suite blending into the color of the room. In his mid-fifties, he was looking extremely handsome. I exclaimed "Dada!" and he stood up with a mischievous smile on his face, as if his purpose to surprise me was served. He embraced me with a lot of warm affection. It was very unusual for him to do that, pretty much against his nature. I was left with the lingering effect of that embrace, wondering if he is happy to see me doing this *Chilla*! Is this how we can please our Gurus, our ancestors?

My body and mind are definitely becoming lighter. All the physical discomforts or even concerns are disappearing. A couple of days ago, when the pain was severe, I had tried to reach the masseuse. I called her a few times; she didn't answer and I took that as an indication. I had thought of taking a pain killer, but refrained from it.

The body is gradually understanding and cooperating with the mind. No intoxicating supplement at all. I never had any. Well, that is not entirely true. Once in my early youth I took a couple of puffs of Hashish on a sea beach of Bakkhali, a sea resort about four hours from Calcutta, on the Bay of Bengal. It was the night of *Dol Purnima*, a full moon in Spring on which the festival of colors is celebrated. While in rest of India it is known as Holi, in Bengal it is called *Dol*. The sky was illuminated by a glaring full moon, spreading its white veil on the placid sea. I was sitting on the beach with a couple of friends. There was a vague presence of a few romantic couples at a distance. We could faintly hear their voices. We could see some of them going into the sea in the darkness of the night, to add their experience of the night. That is how the energy of youth works. They might have been intoxicated too, you never know. Many of the casualties happen in that way. I didn't care much about the puffs of Hashish; it tasted quite insipid to me. That is dangerous, though! This means that if someone could bring me better tasting Hashish, I could get hooked. Perhaps that is how I developed a liking for Long Island Ice Tea. Long Island Ice Tea has nothing to do with ice tea. It is a very strong alcoholic drink, with five different white alcohols, a shot sour mix topped with cola. Its sweet taste can be extremely deceptive; one needs to be careful about it. So, even though I didn't like Hashish, I had it once for a couple of puffs and that was all I wanted. But, I do drink alcohol. Yet, I don't need it. I barely drink in India. Sometimes, on my way to Calcutta, I may pick up a bottle from the airport, a bottle of something I might have been enjoying in Poland or Italy. Reaching Calcutta I put it in the closet and forget about it. For me it is environmental, not mental. Going back to what I was saying earlier, I have successfully won over all concerns of my physical issues, without any external help. This might be an initial taste of freedom in the real sense.

I have always been aware that if I could stay on a certain thing much longer than I normally do, it would gradually reveal more. And, that's what is happening now.

I realized that I am not fully aware of what day of the week it is. It occurred to me for a moment as a passing thought, a vague clueless reckoning. There are, of course, calculative ways to figure that out. But, my mind at present is not interested to do that. What difference will it make? Nature doesn't reveal any difference between what we call Monday, Wednesday or Sunday. Other animals, insects and trees don't care and may not be even aware of such a concept. I can only roughly tell the time of the day. It is so easy to abandon the conventional sense of time.

As I was getting almost done for the day, I had a breakthrough. I was never pleased with the way my left thumb looked and felt. It always felt a bit strained and awkward. I didn't know what to do about it; almost like a new actor on stage, who doesn't know what to do with his or her hands. As I thought deeply about it with a sincere intention to find a solution, it found by itself a very relaxed and comfortable condition. I didn't need to do anything about it. In consequence, it gave me so much freedom to the entire left hand.

This whole process started out of a swelling desire to get my left hand more active in expression, to add more evocative quality to my music. I wanted my tabla to sing more with emotion. So, with an internal cry for it, I sat down after dinner totally focused on this. I said to myself – 'there has to be a way, and I have to find it'. And, suddenly at one point the suggestion came from within to try that change. I was never convinced about such a possibility. But, I tried and it made such a huge difference. I simply did nothing with the thumb; just let it be as it pleased. And, it was happy hearing that from me.

I was excavating more compositions from the past, which I hadn't played in years. They seem to be quite precious, hard to believe that I composed them so early in my life, some from the early eighties! They were sitting in my books and tapes.

Day 8 : July 18, 2016

I grew up hearing from elders that the continued pursuit of music gradually makes musicians humble. They had examples to adduce their persuasion with. I wonder what happened to that humility! In the present scenario of Indian music such examples are not that easy to find. Once my students at the Manhattan School of Music argued that they didn't see any presence of humility in the demeanor of the successful western musicians from Pop, Jazz and Classical fields, who could otherwise become good examples of such attainment! In India the young students of music confide the same observation with me in private interactions. They see a lot of fake humility, easy to tell. In my own early life I also had the same difficulty - to convince myself with examples that there are transformative possibilities in music to elevate an individual into higher level. Not many such instances are out there today. On the contrary, we find musicians suffering from physical and mental illnesses too early in their lives. Most of those illnesses are caused by different types of self-abuse. There are premature casualties and deaths. They come up on stage noticeably under the influence – not convincing enough to be cited as good examples to follow.

It seems weird to me that I am using the expression 'they', as if I am outside that community. Am I not a musician?

Today I introduced the timer to my practice. Based on the material I chose to work on, I set the timer to different durations, between thirty minutes to an hour. Once the timer was on, the hands could not get off from the tabla. Initially I chose to start at a certain tempo, thinking that I would be able to keep up. But, after a while it started hurting. I slowed down for a while only to use that opportunity to learn how to ease out the pain and heaviness in continuity, make adjustments with them and see them off. Once the pain left, I could gradually fly beyond the starting tempo and continue faster without any difficulty. When the timer went off, I was left with numbness in my wrists and fingers.

For certain materials the timer seemed to be moving too fast; the timer buzz bopped me from a meditative state. But, for others the timer seemed like never-ending. Several doubts came into my mind - perhaps I forgot to set the timer on, maybe I had set at a longer duration by mistake, or perhaps the battery went dead.

These speculations clearly indicated severe fatigue. I was laughing at myself, as I normally do to the plight of my students. I don't allow them to stop; I didn't allow myself to stop either – the same treatment. This way I ended up playing through the day and night until next morning.

It rained pretty hard in the afternoon. There were clouds on the sky, but they didn't make it dark. Earlier in the day it was windy, which had stopped right before the rain came. That is how it always happens, to create some kind of expectancy and add to the importance of what is about to happen – like an advent. Perhaps it was the wind, which blew in all of those rain-clouds. The first few minutes of the rain were pretty casual and unassuming. And then all of a sudden it started pouring. I had the skylight windows open, through which the wind was blowing the rain in, partially uninvited. The childhood memories of the excitement of getting drenched in rain never left my mind. But, realizing that it has already drenched some portions of the carpet and advancing towards my tabla, I got up and shut the windows, meaning no offence. The rain actually didn't mind it at all. On the contrary, it engaged into a lovely conversation with my tabla by coming down more audibly on the glass roof-windows. It was pouring so hard that at some point it drowned the sound of my tabla.

Then came the lightning and thunder. I remember Bella, the white dog of Magdalena, usually barks in argument with the thunder. She might be doing the same now in Josh's house. Zorba doesn't care. Puchkie, the little Yorkie we have at home, feels intimidated by thunder, perhaps imagining an impending danger. Such behaviors by these dogs certainly put a question mark to the British expression 'cats and dogs' related to rain. It is interesting to see how every animal respond so differently to the different aspects of nature, as we do. Perhaps a little education in science could standardize their response patterns.

In course of dumping all the water, I heard the clouds saying to the earth, "This is yours; I cannot hold it for you any longer." Most forms of life out there in the surrounding landscape might be a little overwhelmed, but seemingly happy. Humans, particularly those living in the cities, apparently have a problem with such natural phenomenon like the rain, snow or storm. The only people I have seen benefitting from the rain are the taxi drivers. But, they also don't seem to like it; at least that's what they say when we get into their vehicle. Here, out in nature, it is different. Our preferences, liking and disliking don't matter - nobody gives a damn, as they say in America. These days they have replaced the last word in that expression with something a bit more substantial - an object we get to see mostly in the morning of a lucky day. 'Morning shows the day' – sure it does, particularly if you are over fifty. Hope it is not such a difficult quiz!

After quite some time of heavy downpour (could there ever be an up-pour?), something really funny happened. There came moments when the rain stopped altogether, before pouring again with the same amount of intensity. It happened a few times like this. And, finally when it came down for the last time, the sun missed the signal and had already come out. It struck me as if someone was reaching out for the toilet paper and suddenly realized "oh, I am not done yet".

Later at night I could see the reason for such heavy rain. It wanted to clear up the sky for the moon. It was a full moon- just stepping into *Guru Purnima*. I could see the moon through the skylights from my seat. *Guru Purnima* is a full moon, on which Indians chose to salute the presence of Guru in their lives. In the past few years I have felt increasingly sensitive to the upsurge of energy on such astronomically significant occasions. My sleep gets disturbed by a swell of energy in my body. It is good that I didn't go to bed tonight. Instead, I sent the following email to my disciples and few other close ones:

"Today is *Guru Purnima*, a day we've chosen to celebrate the presence of Guru in all of us.

It is of the highest importance in human life to acknowledge this presence in any form of manifestation. Identified as the source of knowledge and wisdom, remover of darkness, this presence is our only guide towards self-realization, which alone can satisfy the purpose of being born as a human.

I am not missing you. At this moment you are in me, as much as I am in you. The moon is there to connect us all.

May you all find a way to live a meaningful life!

May you all live a life free from regret and apology!

May you all beam as fully and beautifully as the moon tonight!

Om, purnam-adah purnam-idam purnaat purnam-udachyate!

Om, that is full, this is full; this fullness is a projection of that fullness!

In exactly a month's time I shall come out of this *Tapasya**. During these past ten days I have started realizing that this is the true beginning of the new phase of my life – *Baanaprastha***. I have been driven by a force towards this destination. There were many doubts, concerns and obstacles. But, my mind made its way through. In many ways it feels very similar to my *Brahmacharya*, when I was new, fresh and alone in pursuit. I am starting all over again.

---

* *Tapasya* is an intense, austere, meditative process towards asceticism.

** According to ancient Indian philosophy, human life was observed in four segments - study (*Brahmacharya*), family and vocation (*Garhastha*), transition towards retirement (*Baanaprastha*) and renunciation (*Sanyas*).

I am not only fine, but better than I was ten days ago. There is a slight concern that my container may be too small for such enormous joy and bliss! Perhaps there will be an automatic adjustment at some point. I am only a witness.

Om shanti, shanti, shanti!
We need so much of that in human soul! Oh mother earth; please forgive us for all our hostility; one day we will be worthy of you.

PraNam to all of you, blessed souls, my precious ones!
Samir"

Day 9 : July 19th 2016 – Guru Purnima

Samir with his Guru Amalesh Chatterjee

Photo Credit: Samir Chatterjee

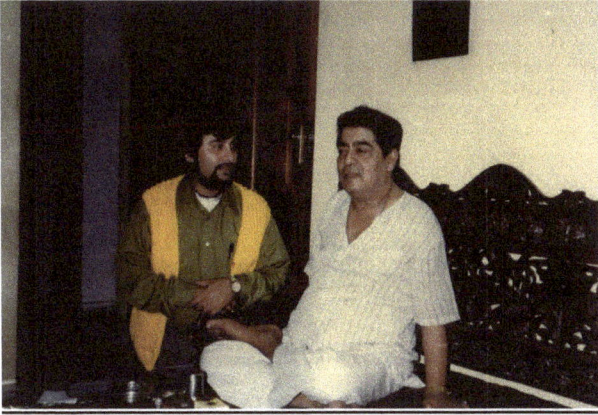

Samir with his Guru Shyamal Bose

Photo Credit: Samir Chatterjee

Today is Guru Purnima, a very special day. I had to make some exceptions. The currents in the flow of communications towards me were very strong. I came online and video conversed with my wife Sanghamitra, son and disciple Dibyarka, disciple Daniel Weiss and a fellow musician Rajyasree Ghosh. Dan, in fact, was free to have a lesson; he was practicing. It was very satisfying to go over some compositions with him. He already knew and remembered most of them from previous lessons. It must have been long time ago; I forgot teaching those to him. But, that is Dan – he remembers every detail of his lessons with me since the inception. He has them documented too.

I had a very meaningful conversation with my soulmate Sanghamitra. It was very different from our regular ones. She was attentive, serious and specific. It felt almost like in our youth, when she used to listen to me with curiosity and interest. Today she wanted to listen more than speaking. So did I, to listen to her more than speaking. I am perhaps losing the habit of talking. The quality of love I saw and heard emanating from her look and voice was revitalizing. It came from her inner self, her true self.

It was hard to get a hold of Dibyarka, but I needed to propose two important additions to our relationship. I wanted to ask for obedience and surrender. It is not easy for a modern young man of his age, intellect and caliber to offer those. They may almost seem like going somewhere blindfolded. I have noticed some willingness in him. He has also verbalized his desire to obey, surrender and be guided by me. Yet, there have also been instances when he showed some resistance. Those put me in doubt, restricting me from my role as a Guru and father. My natural instinct was to withdraw.

The central element in the process of development of a human being is individuality. During that process obedience and surrender are also needed as the two most essential offerings from a disciple to a Guru, particularly in the pursuit of knowledge. Even the propagators of scientific approach to life through questioning and scrutiny wouldn't be opposed to these from their students and followers. If no one was paying any attention to Voltaire, Bertrand Russell, Einstein and Carl Sagan, let alone believing and following them, what would they do? And, if they found someone listening and following, what would be difference? Even non-believers are not free from believing. They also eventually become dogmatic, holding tight to their disbelief.

Later in the evening when I found Dibyarka on video conversation, I asked him if he could give me those two – obedience and surrender. He couldn't give me a straight answer; I didn't expect that either. He would need time to think. Sometimes he doesn't say, but does it. He is very thoughtful. May be he foresees more details of its implications, which makes him cautious. May be he doesn't see that much, and the unknown makes him apprehensive. One thing for sure – he wants to be absolutely certain about his abilities before he commits. His responsible and respectful spirit would never allow him to make a false commitment.

We engaged in conversation, mostly about his internal struggle. He has such a noble heart. Once he had unintentionally hurt a soul, simply out of innocence and ignorance. He came up to me tormented. I suggested him to serve a penance, which he did. But, in doing so, he hurt his mother. Later he served his mother intensely through her prolonged recovery from the first injury. What he did at that time and still continues to do for us is extremely unusual. It brings me so much joy and satisfaction to observe and admire every step of manifestation of the divine in him.

One day driving home from the city I asked him if he would like to join with me in my work in Afghanistan. That day he gave me a straight answer, saying 'Yes". I was a little surprised. I asked him, "Aren't you afraid"? He again promptly responded, "It would be much better to be with you than waiting for your safe return". Watching me on the television performing live on December 12th, 2007 at the Nobel Peace Prize ceremony, he wrote a memorable email to my other disciples. I shall include that here with his kind permission. He titled it as "Presence of Divinity".

"My Guru-Bhais and Guru-Bahens,

Today will remain in my memory 'till my very last breath. I don't know if you were watching CNN this morning (7:30am NY time), but if you did, you know why I say so. I was in a small coffee shop in Newark (NJ) having a quick breakfast before a very busy day. The weather was cloudy and I was staring disinterestedly out of the window at a very dull gray sky. Behind me there was a large screen TV which was tuned to CNN's morning news. Somehow, through my morning stupor I caught the words 'Al Gore' and 'Oslo'; I immediately left the table (my possessions unguarded) and ran to the TV. They were mentioning that the ceremony was running late and that Mr. Gore was expected to give his acceptance within a few minutes. In anticipation of this, they went live to the City Hall in Oslo and to my utter shock I see Guru ji walking on to the stage with Salman Ahmad. They sat down, smiled at each other and after a brief introduction by Salman ji, they began playing. For the next 10 minutes or so (what seemed like an eternity to me), they showed nothing on screen but close zooms of Guru ji and Salman ji, both radiant and glowing. It was a surreal experience! I frantically tried to call everyone I could think of but to my utter disappointment, except for my aunt who caught the last few seconds, no one answered. At that moment you were all I could think about and how this was a moment meant to be shared with you.

I don't know if you know, but tomorrow is the official Nobel banquet where all the celebrity musicians from around the world will be performing. None of them were requested to perform during the actual ceremony today except the two of them. I assume some Indian musicians (Raviji for example) must have been invited to play for the Nobel banquet (concert), but I don't know if any other Indian musician has been requested to perform at the ceremony itself. He was shown a tremendous amount of respect from the moment he arrived, his name was preceded by 'Pandit' in the booklet (he doesn't know where they got that from), his presence there was acknowledged in a special way by the committee and even Mr. Gore himself.

This was the proudest moment of my life, not just as an Indian/Bengali, but also as a son, but most of all, as a disciple. I was thinking about this man's life, where it began, where it has reached, and where it is heading. In a word it can only be described as divine, beyond all other measures of success. After shedding some tears, I walked away to fulfill the day's obligations, but the feeling of awe was overwhelmingly present in my mind and heart all day (it still is). I was determined to write to you, to share a collective experience, to connect with you spiritually. Please call me when you have a spare moment, I need to hear your voices.

Love,
Dibyarko (Dibyarka)

PS: See if you can spot any live broadcast of the banquet/concert tomorrow morning (Tuesday morning here in NY), and if you do, please record it and call to let me know."

Later at night I found a glaring example of obedience and surrender in another person - Rajyasree Ghosh. She was in Calcutta, India. I woke her up at 2.30 am. She could barely talk; needed some time to gather herself. After the exchange of greetings for the special occasion, she delivered the terrible news, which I couldn't rate any less than a disaster. One of the administrators of Chhandayan's West Bengal chapter was causing severe damage to the organization. She was doing that out of dilemma and paranoia, not from any kind of mal-intention. I had asked this administrator to sign and mail a grant application for Chhandayan. Rajyasree reported that she has not only refused to sign the application, but has taken action to stop the entire process and throw away the package I had sent to her from the USA with supporting documents for the application. Before entering the *Chilla* I had explained to her in detail the things she needed to do and trusted her to finish the process. And, there she was, doing just the opposite - taking action towards inaction. It was very upsetting.

I asked Rajyasree to take over the process; to sign and mail the application. Her prompt reply was – "I shall do as you say". She is in her fifties, a professor and musician of very high caliber. In no other area of her life would she be like this. She exudes a very independent and rational personality. She would not accept anything or anybody without having cleared through several levels of security check and rationalization. I am a propagator of free thinking. But, that should not be misconstrued as freedom from obedience and surrender in the learning process. Rajyasree, Dan and few others understand that. Rajyasree is not one of my disciples, not even a formal student. She can, at best, be called an admiring colleague. Yet, the amount of respect and trust I have received from her is immeasurable. This opens up an entire horizon of possibilities. Last year on July 11th, the day of *Guru Purmina*, she wrote an email to me titled *"Guru bole pronam kori jare"* – to whom I bow as my Guru.

Because of her rational approach, she couldn't subscribe to any religious faith, unable to participate in any of their practices. Hence, when she formally entered her new apartment in Calcutta, there was no traditional *Gruha-*

prabesh Puja, a house-warming worship ceremony Indians usually do before living in a new place of residence. All she wanted as an auspicious entry into that apartment was for me to step in first and play tabla. I did that to satisfy her wish. Dan thought that my stepping into his car corrected the failing heating system. Faith and devotion are always to the benefit of those who have them.

This reminds me of a beautiful episode from the Ramayana. Ravana had abducted Rama's wife Sita and taken her to Lanka, which is now called Sri Lanka. Rama set out to rescue her with the help from an army of monkeys. He found them on his way through the south of India. Laugh you may, if haven't seen an army like that. They can rip-off any establishment in no time. They arrived at the southernmost tip of India and, looking at the ocean ahead of them, started wondering how to go to the other side to rescue Sita. Monkeys cannot wait, they are always in action. They started throwing stones into the ocean.

After a few hours of such laborious endeavor Hanuman, the leader of the army and an ardent devotee of Rama, pointed out that there was no trace of any of the stones they had already thrown into the ocean. If they continued like that it would either take them forever or never. They needed to come up with a different plan. They started scratching their heads to open up the pores of intelligence. Hanuman had an idea, not from intelligence, but from his devotion. He started inscribing the name of Rama on a stone, and after touching it to his forehead in salutation, he threw it into the ocean. And, lo - it floated. There was such a moment of joy amongst the army to find such an easy solution. But, it was actually quite a daunting task for Hanuman to do that on every stone before throwing into the ocean. Hanuman didn't think much. He had to get his Rama to the other side. So, he kept on going, like Forest Gump.

The news travelled to Rama about this miracle. He came to visit the site and was astonished to see what was happening. He was agonized too, seeing his devotee at such a painful task. He went up to Hanuman and offered to share some of the work. He proposed that since his name was making the stones float, he himself would stand by the ocean and throw the stones into the water. There was no need to inscribe any more. It sounded logical and Hanuman obeyed, as he always did. He brought a stone to Rama, Rama threw it into the ocean, and it sank. Rama realized that it is not him, but Hanuman's faith in him that made the stones float. Such is the power of faith, trust, obedience and surrender. They may apparently seem like losing acts, because the benefit at the end is not easy to foresee. Rest of the world may ridicule for worshiping a monkey, but this is one of the many reasons why Indians worship Hanuman. He is also worshiped for making impossible possible, through that power of faith and devotion.

We practically have two choices to live a life – with or without. To me both seem equality valid. But, when it comes to methodology, it seems prudent to start with what is already achieved by our predecessors, even to interrogate.

I sent notes to my two Guru-mas (wives of my Gurus) through our nearest connections. I shall call them after August 19th. Other than these interruptions, the day was filled with longer and more enduring practice. Pains and discomforts have moved away. Only thing I noticed is that it is always very heavy in the first few minutes, like starting the ignition of a steam engine. Once it gains momentum, it is smooth and easy on the track.

After yesterday's rain it became chilly all day today. Sanghamitra pointed out that in the recent times I have been susceptible to cold infection. Perhaps I need to have more Vitamin C. I promised to be careful about that.

Day 10 : July 20, 2016

I had written personal notes to two senior stalwart tabla players seeking their blessings. One of them promptly replied with the following message in Bengali:

"THAKOOR tomar mongol koroon. (May you have God's Grace). Pray to THAKOOR to give you mental strength and peace of mind, so that you can complete your mission.

Lots of love and good wishes."

It was from maestro Swapan Chaudhuri.

There is a basil plant in the kitchen by the garden door, it is Magdalena's pride. Three times a day I have been observing it facing me from where I sit at the dinner table. I remember how lively and joyful it was when Magdalena was here. Of late, I don't see that glow in it. It looks sad and morose. It never occurred to me that perhaps it needs water. Outdoor plants are getting enough from the rain. But, this life is reliant on my care, like a pet. I am usually very good at these things. I wonder what is happening to me, where am I mentally? May be there are other plants in the house which need water too.

Tonight's moon is a little mellow. The all whiteness of last night now has a touch of yellow. It is a different beauty, much of which is like the bride after the night of her wedding. In traditional Indian marriage, which is usually arranged, the bride and groom meet for the first time at their wedding. On that night the bride and groom stay up together with friends and family. Usually there is music, recitation or some other kinds of cultural activity. There will also be jokes as interludes, to dispel sleep. This takes place in the bride's house. The following afternoon they go the groom's place. This is that heartbreaking situation, when the girl is leaving her home for good. My father-in-law cried so much while seeing us off that I started feeling guilty of abduction. When he heard me murmuring that to myself, he put a smile on his face appreciating my sense of humor and kissed me on my forehead as a sign of blessing.

On arrival at the groom's place, both of them are received by the groom's mother, with a special welcome to the bride. We all know how it might change a week later. But, at that moment that is the truth. That night the bride and groom sleep separately. This won't make any sense, unless one can see the design. The next day is the reception at the groom's place. On that night they sleep together. She is supposed to stay virgin until that night. The next morning she usually wakes up early, as she is taught by her mother or other elderly women, to defy all speculations – as if nothing happened. But, when she appears out of her bedroom, there is such a stunning beauty in every aspect of her being, which is beyond any description. Words have to stop and watch and feel. She is careful not be noticed. And, if she is noticed, there is an embarrassment and anxiety about being revealed. It's simply ethereal!

There would be a world of difference in the experiences and outlets of these emotions between urban and rural situations. In a city environment she steps out of her room into another room – the bathroom, kitchen or the Livingroom. If there are other people in the house or apartment, there would be exchange of looks and speculations. If she is alone, there is no one to share with. In a rural environment she could run out and share her joy and fulfillment with the sky, the trees, the birds, cows, goats, ducks, dogs or cats – so many of them. Nature is unquestionably a better choice to confide than humans.

In our case nothing really happened. We were married on April 30th and May 2nd in Calcutta was too hot (in a climatic sense), and we didn't have air conditioning. She was tired and exhausted after the rituals and ordeals of the two days. Yet, who would ever forget that night! These are the precious experiences in human life, which can add so much meaning to the whole course. Sometimes I wonder why people fail to appreciate such important things - moments, which do not last or repeat. We get caught up in the social stigma and ignore the ultimate reality of life.

Today I didn't use the timer at all. Instead, I used the metronome and used my internal timer for discipline. One particular type of movement based on the 'dhene dhati ghene' completely slipped away. Every time I approached it, it started hurting so much that I had to stop in caution. It was hurting in the lower hand and wrist areas. I became cautious. This type of rigorous practice routine can easily cause severe and permanent damages to the part of the body in use. Sometimes people overlook or ignore these symptoms while practicing and self-induce damages. One needs to carefully monitor each and every symptom of discomfort. Some of them can and should be pushed further. And, there are some others, which should not be pushed beyond the threshold. A lot of experience and wisdom is needed to make the distinction between the two. I went back to it several times, but it showed the same resistance. Finally, before ending the day, with all the soreness in my right arm, hand and fingers I earnestly appealed to it – "will I not get to see your dance before I go to bed" – and it danced. In joy I played a bit more. Isn't that crazy!

Day 11 : July 21, 2016

This is one of the reasons why I was reluctant to keep this journal. Who cares whether it is day 11 or day 10? But, adhering to my obligatory mentality to share for the benefit of posterity, I conceded. This mentality of sharing was instilled in me by my mother. Since early childhood she whispered in my ears "I am sick and tired of seeing people living for themselves. That is not my son. You will live for others". Later growing up in the environment of Ramakrishna Mission, having Swami Vivekananda as one of my role models, this approach of living for others got further enforced into my character.

During my practice, sometimes I allow my mind to drift away while continuing on a particular type of movement. I want to see whether or not those thoughts and emotions find expression through my playing. If so, how will they manifest. It may not always be fruitful, but very pleasant and satisfying experience, nevertheless. The challenge in this process, however, is to remain present on both tracks. On one hand, I don't want my music to become purely technical and mechanical. And, on the other hand, I need my technique to be at a very high level ready to give me all the freedom and option to express myself to the fullest extent.

The morning practice was very good. I stayed with one particular type of phrase in different combinations and contexts for hours. There were no issues at all. But, when I went back to the same movement of 'dhene dhati ghene', which was giving me trouble yesterday, my right hand started hurting again, at the same places. Hurting would be a soft expression, it started generating excruciating pain. Every time I attempted, it locked me out. It happened several times. Boy, that was tough! I didn't know what to do. I don't give up. I have to create an access into it. Obviously, I started feeling a little depressed, or perhaps concerned is a better way to put it. But, the failure brought in fatigue syndrome. I started dozing off. "Why not take a nap" – I said to myself. Don't know when I fell asleep or when I woke up. But, as I woke up I made a cup of tea and came up with a strategy. I thought of trying the same movement in the middle of some other compositions. And, it worked. This told me that the secret was I just needed to be warmed up to approach her. I say 'her', because to me 'dhene ghene' or 'dhene dhati ghene' both have some sort inherent feminine quality. This feeling evolved out of their tonal emblem, similar to the jingling sound of ornaments.

Vermont is a dairy state. There could be more cows here than humans. However, their social status is very different from their counterparts in India. In India they are worshiped, and here... I don't have to tell you. But, they are raised very well, particularly the ones I can see through my windows. They are grass-fed, meaning cows can be and are fed other things too. During the day, every time I look outside, I see the cows out in the field with their heads down, sincerely grazing. It could be that I have seldom seen a cow out in the field with its head up, except while mooing. This is another type of *Chilla*. All day, every day they are following the same routine. Once out in the field, they know their purpose and never deviate from it. I wonder what kind of life is this! This is what Jonathan Livingston Seagull had denounced.

One evening I was at the Pittsburgh airport waiting for my return flight to Newark, NJ. An 8.30 pm departure was pretty late for that airport. They had built that airport partially as a shopping mall at a time when anybody could walk up to the boarding gate area. Now it looks pretty much deserted. I took a salad from the only place that was open and sat down in the eating area. Except me, there were two other people, two maintenance guys. One of them was sweeping the floor and the other was changing bulbs. Going through my salad I heard the sweeper calling out to his partner – "Man, look at us. You are always looking up, and I am always looking down". It is just by the disparity in their jobs that they were having two different experiences of life.

For a human three things are very important: where you are, who you are with and what you are doing.

Day 12 : July 22, 2016

Since I am practicing round the clock, the counting of days has become a very confusing task; it is very hard for me to differentiate between the end and beginning of days. Sleep has become nap. Today everything was set to the timer, and under deep scrutiny. I slowed down and took a closer look at each and every note. I checked my presence and control over them. It was so embarrassing. I have been playing them for years, yet when I make a proper assessment of my acquaintance with them, I am horrified to see how little I know about them. I cannot forgive myself for such ignorance.

In all honesty, I have always been aware of this and I have always looked for an opportunity of take a closer, magnified or even microscopic look at each and every note, which is part of my music. I really want to know them in as much detail as conceivable - every aspect of them. The more I know them, the more curious I become. To satisfy that increasing curiosity I needed this time and intimacy. I feel blessed to finally have it. I don't know whether it will bring a complete satisfaction at the end of the course. I am not seeking that either. But, at least there will be some partial satisfaction of making an effort.

I feel a lot of pain and tightness in the body when I am not playing. But, once I resume playing I don't feel them anymore. The right index finger has split on the tip. No bleeding yet. I have been careful, applying lotion. But, judging by the number of hours they have been in use, it is not unusual at all.

Day 13 : July 23, 2016

Only a while ago I was seeing some bubble-like figures floating in the air in front of me. They were shaped like illuminated trees, upside down. With the suspicion that I might be hallucinating, I extended my hand to touch them. Most of them escaped, or rather evaporated. There was one courageous shape, which played on my fingertips for a while.

I never had the slightest doubt about the evocative, expressive and transformative qualities in music. Carl Sagan and his colleagues recognized that while preparing the Golden Record for the Voyagers. They chose different samples of music from different human habitations to include in that record as the best specimens of human creations. That is unquestionably the truth. What I wonder about is how much the conventional forms of music and the materials used therein are able to stay in sync with the evolutionary trend of life. If at any point it fails to update itself, it will result in a terrible disconnect between life and music, with dire consequences. Music will fail in its purpose. It is true that certain improvisational forms of music, like Indian classical music, have much greater possibilities to make the necessary adjustments. Yet, in addition to the principles, the basic elements and components of improvisation need to be verified and updated to the relevance in the contemporary times.

Sometimes it seems that the present standard of tabla has surpassed that of the past. It could be true in many ways. Yet, there are also moments, when I have doubt if it is only on a treadmill or actually going somewhere. It is noticeably losing a lot of the sensitivity, which should always be valued as an intrinsic element for any kind of musical expression. It is perhaps not enough only to know the tradition. One needs to follow its continuity from the inception and find the connection between its past and the present. This will help tremendously in establishing its relevance and purpose with confidence. If the contents in use are frozen in time, we need to defrost them and reassess their value before putting them into use.

I have become totally uncertain about which day of the week it is. And, I can broadly tell the part of the day it might be. The sun helps in making an approximation, but not in accuracy. During the summer, particularly during the time before darkness, it could be easily varying by a couple of hours.

I had to put a protection tape on the right hand index finger. It hurts every time I resume.

Day 14 : July 24th, 2016

The hesitant moon

Photo Credit: Samir Chatterjee

It is true that I haven't stepped outside the house in days and have been out of the room only for three times a day, at the most. I have also not spoken a word to anyone. But, these don't mean that I am disconnected from everything. In fact, I am more sensitive and receptive than I have ever been. Perhaps I was like this in my early life, during my childhood and adolescence. Everything I perceive amuses me. Those birds – how they dance and fly; those trees – how they stand still or nod their heads to the wind; the insects in the room – sometimes happy in exploration, sometimes banging their heads on the closed windows. When I try to let them out, they come towards me, forgetting their desire for release. The other day as I was looking out into the night sky, I saw the moon peeping out of a patch of dark cloud. I was wondering why it was so hesitant. Then I noticed a lightening at one end of the sky and understood the reason for its fright. Yet, a few minutes later, when the rain came down I was astonished to see the moon coming out of its hiding – totally dauntless and bold. I don't get to see such things being close to the big city. Perhaps, because of the light we project on the sky such spectacles get covered up from our vision. We don't even know what we miss.

I feel a strange kind of affection towards the little birds, as if they are my grandchildren. It could be just due to their size, and not due to their unknown age. The surrounding sounds that would normally be inaudible or ignored are now magnified to my auditory sensors. And, these wooden houses make a lot of sounds in shifting and adjusting with the change of temperature and humidity. Anyone, who has never lived in such houses, would definitely feel scared about unknown presence, if left alone for a while. Lately I have been expecting to be eye to eye with an owl, which would suddenly appear on the glass skylight window against the dark sky. It hasn't happened yet.

Katha Upanishad* points out that our sense organs are purposefully designed to be outwardly and raises the question what would happen if, by some miracle, they are all turned inward. Will we perceive less, or more? In terms of quantity, it might be less, or perhaps not. But, there would be no comparison in quality.

I saw blood stain on the *Dahina*. I don't know when that happened. But, I put on the protection tape again on the finger before practicing. There was one particular movement in which I slowed down to alternate the middle and index fingers of the left hand. They refused to cooperate. They were repeatedly going back to their earlier habit of making the middle finger, which is naturally the stronger one, do most of the job. It was giving trouble in one particular spot, where I wanted the index to take the lead. It wasn't giving me any consistency at all. It was so annoying. I have been planting the seed for that from the first day of the *Chilla*. It is still resistant in giving me what I want.

On the other hand, that troubling phrase of 'dhene dhati ghene' gave me a prolonged time of consistency and happiness. There were, of course, moments when I was forced to take the right hand off the *Dahina*. But, it gave me two hours of continuity with one short break after the first hour. And, I wasn't taking it easy in terms of tempo and complexity.

---

* Upanishads are a collection of spiritual and philosophical texts.

Perhaps I forgot to mention earlier that I am exercising every day. I have also dipped into the Jacuzzi adding Epsom salt for half an hour twice during the past fourteen days. Those helped a lot.

Day 15: July 25, 2016

Today I was focused on building more strength and stamina. There was no nap, and the rests in between practice spells were less and shorter. One meal was from yesterday's leftover. And, the other was salad, easy to make. Rest of the time I practiced on a series of timers, mostly of two-hour duration. Based on the composition I chose to practice the experiences of time during the timer period, once again, varied between flying and extremely heavy and painful. However it might be, the satisfaction I drew from walking through those courses is uncommon. No doubt this should have been done much earlier in my life. But, it is always better late than never.

I have been dwelling on the human theory of God. We haven't been able to come up with a proper description of this unidentifiable identity. Yet, it has been generously accepted by the entirety of my species. I wonder how necessary that was! Looking at other species we share this planet with, it doesn't seem to be so indispensable. This theory of God was supposed to help mankind out of its sense of insecurity. It sure does, only until it gets into the comparative and competitive arena. At that point the result becomes quite the opposite. It leads only into fragmentations, enmity to the extent of killing each other - all based on the differences in the name of God. Surely there has to be a cause for our annihilation, but why this? We could have easily chosen a different reason. It is perhaps by some miracle that we have not chosen music for such hostility. We have come up with so many different types and forms of music, more than the variety of religions. Yet, we don't have a single instance of people killing each other based on their musical preferences. It only gave human more variety of choices.

Day 16: July 26, 2016

How do you go past intelligence? Words, thoughts and ideas seem like barriers. My consciousness seems to be inescapably caught up in that enclave. It also seems like there is nothing in particular that I can do about it – to surpass intelligence. It is an inherited, inherent quality that has evolutionarily inculcated a lot of pride in my species. Nevertheless, I have had instances in my life when my wish and wait were answered in due course. So, perhaps I can draw assurance from those past experiences that there is hope. My purpose is to go to the center of my perpetual, imperishable being. What it says in that Tagore song my mother was singing on the first day:

> *"Dnaarao aamar aankhiro aage,*
> *tomaro drishti hridaye laage"*

Please stand in front of me, let your vision touch my soul.

- perhaps it doesn't work that way. It doesn't come and stand in front of us. We have to make our way to it, with purity and humility. Purity always seems to be such a vulnerable concept to me, assessed by social, cultural, ethical and religious standards of morality. I prefer to think of it as something close to my unconditioned self, what I would refer to as my Natural Self, the one I was born with. It can only be matured, but not compromised. Isa Upanishad assures that Self to be unstainable. It is, then, left to our ability to perceive it that way in our consciousness. This is what I would like to bring into my music – the perception of that Self. That is what this is all about – these forty days, those in the past and those in the future.

The practice from the last couple of days seems too dry compared to today's. I don't know exactly what caused this difference. It is perhaps because I stopped using timer. The timer definitely took me to a dry zone, like walking through a desert. Sometimes there can be excitements. But, for the major part, it is all just dry sand all around me in different shapes and shades. It is a test to perseverance. I like it a lot; doesn't permit any sort of self-indulgence. But, it seems also necessary to go back to the strong and ultimate presence of the human element in me.

Day 17: July 27th, 2016

Isn't it interesting to notice how the day and date have been ten numbers apart!

I definitely need a combination of mechanical and intellectual practice. When I find something to work on, it usually springs out of my intellectual activity. But, when I start working on it, I need to be absolutely headlong mechanical. I need to dive into it free from the trend of improvisatory thoughts. That, in a sense, is surrender.

Today, sometime in the late morning or early afternoon, I realized that my mind is in a very strange state. It is neither happy, nor sad, neither energetic nor depressed. It is not black or white or grey. There are lots of colors. Yet, it is very still and tranquil.

Today I introduced a new thing to my practice – a tempo chart. I listed the drills and compositions I have been focusing on almost regularly. I played them for their usual duration and noted down their highest levels of sustained tempi. This might be useful later to see the progress or none.

Day 18: July 28, 2016

The day slipped away in wilderness- to nothingness. I don't know how that happened, can't explain. I started with motivation. I had a new strategy - to start differently, with the compositions I was practicing later in the days. I felt I was practicing them when my energy might have been ebbing down. So, I flipped the choice of materials around and it went well for some time. But, then towards the middle of the day it became hard to go back to the basic drills. That is when things started falling apart. I struggled and was able to regain some of the energy. But, at some point, I had to let it go. I am not regretful, maybe I am. May be it is not about feeling good or bad, or being satisfied or not. Perhaps I am on a plateau with no ups or downs. We will see; I have a tomorrow.

Day 19: July 29, 2016

I don't know where I am going, or if I am going anywhere at all. I cannot find my usual sense of satisfaction anywhere around. I am not feeling hungry or sleepy. I am putting in more hours simply out of a sense of discipline, or perhaps I have chosen nothing else to do. It is like being in a desert, where the only sense of direction one can draw is from the stars; but only when they are visible. Or, I am in a space, where there is no definite sense of east, west, north, south, up or down, except from the perspective of my physical form. What if my true self comes into prominence, making the physical form secondary! In the midst of all these placid mental states, there are possibilities of losing so many things I have been attached to as helpful means to living.

There were three spells of three hours of continuous playing and a few more of shorter duration. During those spells I shifted my right leg position a couple of times or finally stretched it ahead. But, my hands didn't get off. I had to take short breaks after each three hours. Without those, my hands didn't want to move. Every start was like that of a beginner. The main weakness is in my left hand. It feels imbecile. However hard that is, I had to accept and work on it. There are so many materials to practice that a day seems way too short even to touch upon. So, the best idea, perhaps, is not to worry about day, time or anything at this point and keep going.

All day there was a tremendous urge to call my wife and friend Sanghamitra.

Day 20: July 30, 2016

I moved my seat closer to the wall in order to hear more bounce back of my sound. With a thick protection tape on the tip of my index finger, I am not getting the full satisfaction of my right-hand tone. Also, on most of the days, it has been pretty humid between 11 am and 5 pm. That dampens the *Bayan* sound quite a bit, which makes it even harder to draw enough tonal inspiration. I have to generate all inspiration from within. Sometimes I find the right tone and feel motivated to hold on to it. It seems like a door is opening and I keep going. Sometimes it seems like I am at a dead end, nowhere to go. And, I still keep going.

I don't know what the cows are doing, where the birds are. It seems like nature has been standing still by me. Occasionally I hear some sound, which I cannot relate to. They are there. I am somewhere else, engrossed in my own space.

There is not much of an appetite. Still I made some breakfast – toasts and eggs. There is a little bit of an anxiety about being able to finish some of the grocery Magdalena had stacked up for me. It would be impossible to finish it all. But, what I realized in making and having food is how much it can revitalize my energy. It also felt as part of the larger spectrum of discipline. We perhaps don't eat only to satisfy hunger and draw nutrition. It is a habit and discipline. Not all the food we eat might be that necessary; and there are, of course, the ones we consume for pure pleasure. But, food serves other purposes too. The entire process involved in the planning and execution of food serves an immense motivational purpose.

I often refer to this significant episode from Buddha's life. He was sitting under the banyan tree for days and nights meditating for Nirvana. Nothing was happening, except that his body was turning into a skeleton. One day a young mother came out from the nearby village with a bowl of rice pudding. It was perhaps her son's birthday. She was looking for someone really in need of food to make an offering. She found this skeletal man under the banyan tree, meditating. With all her devotion, she placed the bowl in front of the man and went back to the village. The smell of food and a sense of human presence interrupted Buddha's meditation. He opened his eyes and found the bowl of rice pudding. It was delicious. He finished it in no time and went back to mediation. And, we all know what happened after that – Nirvana! I wonder who told that story. Must have been Buddha himself. No one else was presumably around to witness. That village girl Sujata had already left.

In my adolescence and early youth, I was deeply involved into intellectual activities, delving into the wide variety of ideas and 'ism's from Asian and European thinkers and writers. New ideas, new ways of looking at life fascinated and engulfed my mind. At that time food became secondary in consideration. Any discussion on food for more than a minute seemed not only irrelevant, but also gross. I used to react severely against such petty talks. I thought we eat only to live. I don't know when that flipped to the opposite notion that we live to eat. Perhaps Sanghamitra brought that change in me. She brought in so many other significant changes, she doesn't even know.

Day 21: July 31, 2016

Samir and Sanghamitra at Lake Shrine, California

Photo Credit: Swami Nikhilananda

It is interesting that my notes on two consecutive days ended with Sanghamitra. I wonder why. What is it between the two of us! Is it just the eternal Man and Woman relationship or there is something more in it! When I try to think of us in terms of just Man and Woman, it doesn't really satisfy me as a complete explanation. The Man and woman aspect in the relationship primarily focuses on the two physical forms, with their own nature and needs, such as shelter, money, security, food, physical attraction, etc. Some of these might have been present in the beginning of our relationship. But, what we have now between the two of us is far beyond those elements. I wonder if we have unknowingly transcended that baseline and elevated to a slightly higher level.

There has been an incident in our lives in recent times, which we will never forget. It reaffirms my assumption that it is no longer limited to the 'demand-supply' explanation. Late on the evening of February 20th of this year, 2016, Sanghamitra had an accident. She was brought down by a motorbike on a main road in Kolkata, formerly Calcutta. She was alone waiting for a bus. The handle of a motorbike got entangled with the handle of her shoulder bag. She fell and broke her right hip ball so badly that it needed a replacement, which was surgically done the next afternoon.

In parts of December and January all three of us were together in Kolkata. I had to return on January 19th to catch up with my semesters in the USA. My son Dibyarka returned ten days later and went back to work. Sanghamitra stayed back, scheduled to return on February 28th. Stuck here with our own works, my son and I had no possibility of taking any more time off to go back to Kolkata. It was a painful situation at both ends. Our only option was to monitor the entire process of treatment electronically. Everything went well and she was released from the hospital on the 24th. She returned to our Kolkata apartment and was settling down for recovery.

February 20th was a Saturday. On Tuesday I was on road returning from Pittsburgh. The landscape in certain parts of that highway route is breathtaking. Even after seeing them for so many times, I draw a lot from them - the mountains, forests and the sky. Looking at them my heart started yearning for her. I decided to drop everything and go back to Kolkata to be with her. I had to wait until that Friday to complete a contractual agreement and on Saturday morning I took a flight. She didn't know I was coming.

Rajyasree picked me up from the airport and took me home. She first entered the apartment and two of them engaged in their usual conversation. I creeped in quietly and stood in front of her at the door. Looking at me she felt shocked and started crying. She cried non-stop for fifteen minutes, to the point of choking and throwing up. To feel such swell of emotions for one another is not that common. We were both sixty one years old, acting as if we were sixteen. It was apparent to me that no one needs to be perfect or in compliance with each other's preferences. It is pure love. After two weeks, when I had to return to the USA leaving her alone to recover, we were both wondering whether it was a good idea for me to visit her like that. The pang of separation made us numb, as it did thirty eight years ago.

The practice in the morning was very intense and organized. I didn't set up the timer.

Instead, I relied more on my internal discipline. It felt good. I was able to cover most of the materials throughout the day. Magdalena returned in the afternoon with the dogs. The atmosphere in the house changed radically. We had dinner together with rice and some dishes I had cooked. And, we chatted about her trip. Then I went back to practice as she continued with some gardening work.

Day 22: August 1, 2016

Today is the first day of August and it is cloudy. There is an ancient epic poem written in Sanskrit by Kalidasa. The third line of that poem begins with "on this first day of *Ashara*, the sky covered with clouds....". In India *Ashara* is the first of the two months of monsoon. The poem is titled '*Meghadootam*', which would literally translate to 'cloud messenger'. It is funny to observe that even in this age of technology we are still using cloud for messaging. In that poem a young man was banished from his land for ignoring his duties. He was newly married, too absorbed in the thoughts of his wife. So, the banishment came more as a punishment by separating the newly married couple than the apparent geographical displacement of the young man. While in exile, taken over by the pang of separation, one day the young man noticed a bunch of passing clouds, flying towards his homeland, where his wife was. He started beseeching the clouds to take his message of love to his wife. May I use these

Vermont clouds for the same kind of favor - to take my message of love to Sanghamitra in Nutley, New Jersey?

Before coming to Vermont I was touring Europe for almost a month. When I came back home for two weeks before leaving again for Vermont, Sanghamitra sat down with me asking about this *Chilla*. She was mainly concerned about the fact that I shall be completely out of her reach, cut off from all communications. What if something happens to me! I told her that if something really happens to me, she should be the first person to feel and know about it. I suggested that we should both work on strengthening our internal connections. She went quiet. I know exactly how much my silence in these past twelve days has been tormenting her. It is the speculative mind. What I said to her on the night before I started the *Chilla* was brutal – "Imagine this to be a trial to live this life in my absence". Although in many of our private conversations I have promised to live beyond her, yet life is so predictably unpredictable.

I have detected some vague and uncertain areas in some of the compositions I usually play. I located those areas by repeatedly slowing down and pausing at different areas through the compositions. Once I am able to spot them, I start digging deeper into them in an uncompromising way. This has some similarity with planting. We dig to loosen and clean up the soil before sowing or planting. This brings in the optimum result. It is a mammoth undertaking. In addition to being analytical and critical, one also needs a lot of patience. I am actually resetting several techniques and touches, almost like relearning them. I have earlier played through them a million times. But, there was always a sense of incertitude and imperfection. This wide-open time-span and non-distracted mental state is allowing me to work on those areas patiently and intensely. Apart from the release from time-pressure, I also have much less concern about the outcome. All I am trying to do is make an honest attempt. It is not so much about speed as it is about clarity and expression. One thing I am realizing more and more - that the lead may not be so much in looking for new materials, but in finding freshness in the existing ones.

Day 23: August 2, 2016

There is a state of the mind, which is beyond black and white. It is not even grey. On the contrary, it has all the colors humanly perceivable. I had an experience of that during my practice earlier in the day. It just took over my entire consciousness. I was perceiving nothing else. It superseded my habitual perceptions through the senses. I was playing, but I was hearing more than what I was playing. I was hearing the sound of colors. My eyes were open from time to time. But, it didn't matter. All I was seeing was an array of colors. My sense of touch transcended all of the sensory experiences and converted them to colors. There was neither happiness, nor sadness. There was no relevance of those in that state of my mind. I cannot tell how long I stayed in that state. It was not possible to hold on to those moments or any particle of those colors; it won't allow. But, I am trying to document the experience as fresh and as accurately as I am able to, before my memory returns to the ordinary.

As I went back to practice those colors started radiating, becoming brighter and brighter until I realized that it was the Sun – the Sun I couldn't look at for more than a few seconds as it came out of the Southern Rim of the Grand Canyon. The brightness of that is incomprehensible. Yet, it is so soothing. I never knew it could be perceived in such a unique combination. My body, my mind, my entire being feels blessed, taken over by this unique presence. This cannot be described as happiness. It is a feeling of awe, which is pervading over all other emotions. I don't know if I would like to, or need to see more. I feel no such immediate urge. I didn't even expect this. I don't know whether this came from outside or generated from within. But, it is certainly a reality.

Rest of the day went by wondering about it.

Day 24: August 3rd, 2016

This morning I looked strange and unfamiliar to me in the mirror, as if I was looking at someone else's image.

Like any other repertoire, tabla also has certain compositions, which are meant only for those who are serious into practice. Those who practice less may appreciate them, but will be ditched if they try to play those compositions. They also have an alternative – to fake. That seems to be working well for many, but not for me. To me that option is similar to lying, trying to prove false as the truth. For me pursuit of truth, in this context, has three levels:

a) to stay true to the language. Tabla has a highly developed drum-language. Everything played on the instrument is connected to its language. Compositions are developed using that language. My attempt is to play exactly as it is in the language, spelling and pronouncing every word and syllable with clarity and control.

b) If my finger is touching and playing a note, I need to be fully aware of that; it shouldn't be left to habitual action.

c) I would like to have control over those touches and strokes as much as possible. It is similar to having a relationship with every organ in my body, to the point of being able to regulate them.

Talking about truth and falsehood, one of our professions is designed to present false as truth. People spend a lot of money to gain and hire that proficiency. It is bewildering to see how and how far things get compromised as we live on. That could be one of the reasons for our accumulating sense of guilt along with maturity. In the early stages of our lives we are taught not to lie. Later in adolescence we are intrigued by observing those teachers of truth, mostly our parents, lying. When we ask, we are explained that a little lie here and there for greater cause is okay. And then, finally in youth we are sent to an expensive school to become an expert in lying professionally.

To remain truthful is one of the hardest challenges of human life. Sometimes, even after knowing that we are not being truthful, we manipulate and try to misinterpret facts in self-defense. In our social, political and economic ideologies we had originally intended to uphold truth. But, in setting up the methods of execution, we deliberately kept many loopholes to take advantage of towards making convenient compromises.

Day 25: August 4th, 2016

In the morning I went down to the kitchen to have a cup of coffee with Magdalena. That's when I came to know that today was her birthday. We talked a little bit about our personal memories of different birthday celebrations. I also had some eggs and toasts with coffee. I came up to practice and she went to work. It went well until noon. And then it started dragging. The combination of heaviness and pain gradually took over and knocked me out. After some struggle I decided not to give in. I ate a small lunch and took a nap setting the alarm. I woke up, did some stretching, took a shower and went back to practice. It was much better. I had my body and mind together.

Magdalena came back from work. Since I couldn't take her out for dinner, I tried several delivery options. There was none available in this area. So, I had requested her to pick up some of her choicest dishes on her way back. We had that for dinner. We chatted a little more after dinner. I decided to call it a day. I am going to bed at 11 pm setting up the alarm at 3 am.

Day 26: August 5, 2016

Good morning! I just finished practicing one type of phrase called 'dhere dhere' for three hours. I was approaching it from different angles, changing perspectives through different combinations of phrases and tonality. I was using dynamics as well, all towards more expressiveness. In my practice I am seldom casual. Once warmed up, I go up to a reasonable tempo, where I can test my stamina and control. The overall feeling is that of calmness, with an inner current of jubilation.

There were definitely moments when I wanted to stop or even check the timer. Who was going to check on me or blame me if I yielded to those temptations? Three hours is a long spell of time, particularly at a high level of tempo. Apart from the soreness, there was sweat all over my body, starting to itch in certain parts, a couple of insect bites and call for toilet. Any of these could have been chosen as a justified reason to stop. But, I didn't.

It is always such a good feeling to greet the Sun. I could also see the Sun reciprocating by caressing the trees, grass and everything around with so much affection. It does the same at the end of day. It is similar to the way humans are treated with delicacy and affection at the beginning and end of life.

I went back to practice after a break for half an hour. My fingers had gone numb after those three hours of continuous 'dhere dhere' practice. I resumed with the standard 'terekeTe' *Rela*, another fast composition, and got locked out after 40 minutes. I felt like I was having an iron ball inside the deltoid muscles of my right upper arm. Once again hit by fatigue and doziness I took a coffee break.

Magdalena had to take her car to the shop. Since it was a quick trip for an hour and half, she left the dogs in the house. I went back to practice and Zorba took his position on my bed. Bella decided to take to barking. When it comes to barking, Bella knows her business very well, like those nonstop crying babies in the nonstop flights. But, this was different from her usual alarm barking sensing intrusion or activities in the property. She was missing her mother. She is only two years old. Zorba, as the senior, felt concerned and started looking outside the window trying to speculate on Magdalena's return. Somehow he understood that this was going to be quite a while. He went back to my bed with his head up turned towards Bella, who sounded like somewhere outside my door, still barking. Bella doesn't come this far into my room. Perhaps she sees a barrier, which Zorba doesn't. Bella was barking nonstop, with occasional pauses. Those pauses were even worse than continuity, because they brought in false hope that she has stopped. But, in reality she was only taking a breath or adjusting her jaws before resuming. I couldn't get up to console her, because I was on timer for 80 minutes. Zorba tried to pacify her with the assurance of his presence. But, he couldn't sacrifice my company for that. The best he could do was to sit right outside my door offering his presence to Bella with his head up, having me in his sight. But, it didn't help the situation a tad; it meant nothing to Bella. So, feeling disappointed, he returned to my bed. But, he couldn't be as comfortable as he normally is. After about 50 minutes of such disturbance, he makes his final move. He went out to Bella and rubbed his nose against her. I don't know what exactly he said to her. But, Bella went absolutely quiet until Magdalena returned.

That coffee helped a lot. I thought I would need a nap in the afternoon. But, it doesn't look like that. It has been seven hours so far. And, I am feeling fine. In continuity, something interesting happens. At the lowest points, when I am seemingly exhausted and feeling like I cannot go any further, I either slow down or go a little softer trying to relax my muscles. And, then suddenly I find something new in tonality or phrasing and feel reenergized. The fatigue I was feeling earlier moves away until the end. So, I have decided not to be conclusive too soon. Instead, wait and see what happens. It is definitely worth the endurance.

Since I am using the timer, I decided to introduce a practice chart and log in the hours I am putting into each material. Today's entries added up to fourteen hours between 3 am and 11 pm. I am wondering what happened to rest of the hours in between. Perhaps the breaks were too long. Tomorrow I shall try to recuperate within lesser time.

Day 27: August 6th, 2016

At 5.24 am this morning I got electrified from the *Dahina*. I cannot explain what happened and how it happened. But, I shall try to briefly describe what I felt; I have to return to my practice. I was practicing the 'dhere dhere' Rela. And suddenly I felt an electrical shock on my right hand index fingertip, moving like a flash of lightening up the hand to the upper arm. In a momentary thought, it occurred to me that the *Shyahi* (the black circle) on the *Dahina* has some metallic elements in it, such as iron dust. May be out of friction...! I wasn't wearing the protection tape this morning. The air is quite a bit humid - a little drizzle outside. I am sure there would be some scientific explanation of such sudden occurrence. But, even the science of physics or neurology may have hard time explaining in simple terms why such things don't happen all the time, or cannot be replicated at will.

This shock was very different from the common feeling of static electricity. This is like putting your finger inside a 220 volt power socket. It didn't numb my hand, but put it in an unusual state with a tinge of burning sensation. I had to stop for a moment - the common response to electrical shock. Then I tried to continue, waiting to see what happens next. After a while, I felt something bubbling up within – some sort of energy! I took a short break to scribble down on my notebook. I am now struggling to go back to practice. My mind is in a slightly ecstatic state, not yet settled down. May be it will in a while.

A little later I bumped into a section in the book 'The Bhagavat Gita According to Gandhi'. *Bhagavat Gita* means a discourse from *Bhagavan* or God Krishna. In this section Gandhi was dealing with *Raaj Yoga*, translated as the Sovereign *Yoga*. Gandhi's translation of verse 40, as spoken by Shri Krishna to Arjuna, is "Here no effort undertaken is lost, no disaster befalls. Even a little of this righteous course delivers one from great fear."

Gandhi comments on this saying "No sin is incurred by those that follow the path of action. A beginning made is not wasted. Even a little effort along this path saves one from great danger. This is a royal road, easy to follow. It is the sovereign *Yoga*. In following it, there is no fear of stumbling. Once a beginning is made, nothing will stand in our way.

This is a very important verse. It contains the profound idea that nothing done is ever lost, that there is no sin in the path of action. This is the royal road. This path is the path of Truth. There is no harm, no fear of destruction, in following it."

The next verse says "The attitude in this matter, springing, as it does, from fixed resolve is but one, O Kurunandana; but for those who have no fixed resolve the attitudes are many-branched and unending."

Gandhi's comments on this are "The resolute intellect here is one-pointed. Along this path one must hold one's intellect so firm that there is no wavering. The actions of a man whose intellect is not fixed on one aim, who is not single-minded in his devotion, will branch out in many directions. As mind leaps, monkey-fashion, from branch to branch, so will the intellect.....It does not help us to realize the *Atman**. In fact, we lose our soul. We lose our *Dharma*, we lose the capacity for good works, lose both this world and the other."

It is so strange – as if this passage was waiting there for me to read and find an explanation for this unusual occurrence. It is once again from the *Baghavat Gita*. And this

---

* *Atman* is the Sanskrit word for soul.

Dahina I am playing on is associated with that *Bhagavat Katha* of the Raritan Center, New Jersey. My mind is naturally finding these connections.

I came to know from Magdalena that today is Saturday; she doesn't have to go to work. Saturday is supposedly dominated by the planet Saturn. Romans called it *Sāturni dies* or Saturn's day. I was born on May 26th and the predominant planet for that day is the Saturn.

Day 28: August 7, 2016

We are better than what we think of ourselves. But, we don't know. That has been such a major issue with my kind. What sits at the center of Self-Realization is this awareness – the awareness of what we are, who we are. This quest involves far more than the understanding of the materialistic properties of the Self. It is a full and complete qualitative assessment of the Self that alone can satisfy a seeking human. Being involved in that process, we come to realize how individualized the journey is and has to be.

There is a question raised in the *Upanishads*: how do you know something that is already known to you. The starting point to find an answer to that question would be in seeing the fine line between what is considered to be unknown and can aspired to be known. Yet another puzzle! How do you even guess the unknown? One needs at least a few experiences in life to allow the conjecture that things are not as they often seem to be. I am not what I often think I am. If that thought of doubt ever creeps into our consciousness, it is a good start. Having that doubt and conjecture may take forever, or never.

Once that conjecture matures into inquisitiveness, we can start the journey. People who have some experience of walking through that path may follow their intuition. But, for others, it would be a good point to find a guide often known as the Guru. The Guru knows the way and is a little ahead in the course. Finding the Guru should create a possibility to see the All Good in us and keep us steered away from darkness. Sometimes darkness plays a deceptive game in convincing us as it's opposite. It is quite dangerous! Experienced people playfully handle it like a snake charmer. Less experienced people may get bitten. This is one of the many hurdles in that journey. Having a guide at these initial stages seems quite prudent to me this morning, as things suddenly started appearing in a very simplistic way.

Some moments of privacy in isolation might help to see more of that revelation. Perhaps that is why seekers go out – to find or create moments for our true self to express and reveal itself. A little moment won't convince privacy and isolation, it needs a stretch of time and opportunity. There also has to be a genuine interest in seeing and knowing more. With this assurance the All Good in us reveals. Blessed will be those, who get to see the true and complete nature and quality of the source of the manifested Self. That is the true realization of our Selves. It is free from mysticism.

Day 29: August 8, 2016

This is my extended honeymoon with tabla. We have been married for so long. But, we never had a chance to step out like this. Tabla couldn't do much about it, except waiting. I had to take the initiative. It is such a different experience being just the two of us with such intimacy for an extended period of time. The subtleties and nuances of tabla can unfold only under such conditions. Some of the many aspects and qualities revealing now were already known to me, but compared to my present experiences, I won't rate that knowledge to be any more than merely theoretical or partial. To have them for real in such overwhelming abundance is entirely different.

A few years after our marriage, Sanghamitra started feeling a little jealous when the proportion of her shared time with tabla inclined a little too heavy towards her opponent. Quite often she observed tabla taking over my entire day. That's when Sanghamitra started considering tabla as her rival sister-wife or co-wife, both of them poor translations of the Indian word *'Sauten'*. The word most likely has its origin in Arabic language. Indian romantic songs are infested with this word *Sauten* in expressions of jealousy in love.

Sanghamitra and I were both young at that time, living in our Calcutta apartment. She used to spend a lot of her morning time in the kitchen, as she still does. Between her position in the kitchen and my seat in the music room we had a clear view of each other at work across the living-dining room. Both of us enjoyed having each other in sight in our own individual ways. Yet, there were moments when tabla would tempt me to show some places I have never been before. When I heard the whisper from tabla, I looked for some privacy. I would get up and close the window and door of my music room to the living-dining room. Eventually, engrossed in my intimate moments with tabla, I would be totally oblivious of my surroundings and forget how unbearable it might have been for Sanghamitra. After a while, she would suddenly irrupt, flying open the window and door announcing "I need to see you". I would naturally get startled by such abrupt intrusion, yet never failed to appreciate her expression of love. Tabla, on the other hand, couldn't say anything against such interruption of intimacy. It kept hanging on to me. Now tabla seems to be happy that after all these years I have been able to curb out some real time with her. According to the laws in most human societies, having a second wife may be considered illegal and immoral. But, the governing law here in such romantic domain is somewhat different. It teaches a relationship of not only tolerance, but mutual love and affection. I don't see tabla having an issue with that. Rest is all up to Sanghamitra.

I know that it has been extremely difficult for Sanghamitra, as it has been for me, to remain unseen and silent like this to one another for such a prolonged period of time. Even when I came out to the west on tour or went to Afghanistan, some possibilities of communication were always open. During this period I had to shut everything off. So, there were a couple of times when my spiritual responses to her agony weren't enough; I had to call her. And, when I did I found her crying on the other end. Blessed be her soul for such love. Blessed am I to have her in my life.

During or after our conversation on the phone, she asked if the accuracy of the timing of my calls was mere coincidence. I responded by saying that "there is no coincidence" and explained later with this follow-up note:

> "You must be wondering about what I meant by saying "there is no coincidence". You are a simple person. So, rather than leaving you wondering and wandering with tiring and confusing guesswork, I shall explain to you in simple terms. But, please read through every word carefully.
>
> All our ideas and efforts of developing communication sprang from our past experiences, mostly out of our ability to communicate from the gross to the finest levels. These communications have

pervaded human life from the inception. What it entails is opening up channels for information to flow through and connect with one another. These connections may end up in blending or collisions. Obviously, the consequences of the two would be diametrically opposite. In the spectrum of infinite time, it doesn't really matter. But, momentarily it does.

So, if the channels of communication between the two of us are open and functional, then they have a strong possibility of transmitting and receiving information, such as thoughts and feelings. Depending on the compatibility or incompatibility of the two sources, the information passing through may blend or collide. In our case, I have kept my channel open, backed up by an awakened state of my mind. Any information coming this way is immediately detected and monitored. If my channel is not monitored, the information will go ignored and unattended. And, if the channels are not open, then there will be nothing passing through. It is all within human abilities to do these at will."

Talking about honeymoon, I realize that I shall be seeing another full moon at the end of this *Chilla*, probably on the 17th or 18th of August. When I chose the dates for *Chilla*, I didn't think about it.

Something interesting has become apparent. Since that incident of electrification on August 6th, I haven't felt any kind of heaviness or pain in my right arm or hand. I noticed that yesterday and I was allowing some more time to be confirmed about it. Late morning till early afternoon is still the hardest. I am dozing off, needing a nap. So, today I sat on the couch and took a short nap for 20 minutes. Other than that it was relatively easy to continue. There were, of course, a few down points, but endurable. The highest point, however, is between 4 and 6.30 am. I am waiting for that time tomorrow.

Zorba has started spending the night on my bed. He has surpassed the gender connotation of love. He is a male and me too. So what?

Day 30: August 9th, 2016

This morning at 3.30 a.m. I started practicing with a lot of freshness and enthusiasm. But, about an hour and half later I noticed that enthusiasm gradually ebbing down. And, at around 6 am nothing seemed to be working anymore. I was still playing, but only mechanically; my mind wasn't there. Despite all sincere attempts to stay awake and alert, I was repeatedly going into slumber. Every attempt to stay awake would work only for a few minutes before I dozed off to indifference. I had to recognize and acknowledge this as dead end and, out of respect to my body, gave in to take a nap. When I woke up, I took some breakfast, which made me fresh and energetic as ever, ready to resume. As a result, it became a very different late morning experience than any previous ones during this *Chilla*.

The choice of materials to practice at a particular time has been mostly prompted from within. I hear before I play. Sometimes, when there is no such natural prompt, I have to make a conscious selection. That selection may or may not work; I have to keep myself open to both possibilities. The opportunity to learn and practice, free from any kind of pressure and comparative judgement, has been the biggest benefit of being in this process. There is nothing to be proven or adhered to.

Finding areas to work on is neither easy, nor difficult. Some of the problems are quite obvious, easily detectable and rectifiable through some attention and honesty. There are also problems, which are slightly more difficult to detect. They need a little bit of a stir to be popped up. In frequent passages through certain phrases I might have always felt somewhat uncertain and awkward. What I have now is the opportunity to recognize those discomforts as indications of some underlying issues in one or more notes in those phrases. I am benefiting from my own matured discerning ability, which is raising the suspicion. If one doesn't have that ability, he or she can seek advice from someone trusted, respected and allowed access. That's the only way to make this detection and rectification process effective.

There is yet another type of problem, which is extremely difficult to detect and rectify. They usually reside at a much deeper level, almost impossible to detect. Their places of hiding are apparently so innocent and covered up, that common eyes and ears would not raise any suspicion. The detection, exposure and treatment of those problems would be much more intense than the ones previously mentioned. To set up the mind to deal with these issues, the 'feel good' mentality has to give way to the 'do it right' attitude. It has to come out of the conviction that no matter what it takes to fix the problems, there will be inevitably more beauty at the end – the beauty of perfection. We don't need to worry about the beauty of imperfection; there will always be room for it.

Once these deep-rooted problem areas are spotted, a special treatment is needed to force the issues out, almost in the same way we force out something hidden in a cave or a hole. We usually set out a fire and blow some of the smoke into those innocent looking holes or caves. In the same way selecting the phrases in suspicion and looping them over and over in varied levels of tempo would inevitably reveal the spots of weakness and imperfection. What might have seemed all right earlier in the passing may now explicate flaw. Some musicians feel joyous with the success in finally being able to locate the flaw; they immediately start working on them with utmost sincerity. Yet, there are others who might be hit by severe frustration and despair. To acknowledge the fact that what was considered to be known and done is not yet fully known or done is a humongous challenge for them. A lot of patience, self-counselling, spiritual strength and physical stamina are needed to survive through this process. It would be extremely helpful to remember that it is ultimately going to be to our own benefit. We cannot and should not indulge in any escapist mentality. Such childish pampering doesn't take us anywhere. What is to be done is to be done, no escape.

Once the material is chosen and the methodology to work on it is determined, there needs to be an unwavering confidence that if we do the right thing in the right way, the result has to be good, whatever that might be. It might take us to a place we never thought of being in.

The benefit of this search and clean-up is manifold. It not only gives us clarity and control through the analytical exercise of breaking down and zooming in from larger to smaller areas and the reverse, it also yields new perspectives to the notes and phrases under spotlight. Fresh ideas to use them in different melodic, rhythmic and compositional contexts automatically pop up. Notes and phrases are merely tools for expression. Just as our emotions and experiences are varied in range, so are the possibilities in the utilization of these tools. The practice of music should ideally help us in developing the compatibility between the two.

Whether we are working on our own compositions or others should not matter. Every time I hear my compositions performed by others, I find a new perspective. It could be very different from how I thought about it while composing. In fact, with the passage of time, I may not even remember what exactly my thoughts and feelings were at the time of creation. It is now an opportunity to take a fresh look at it.

Day 31: August 10, 2016

In the past 30 days I have been not only resetting many of the technical and tonal aspects of my playing, but I am also questioning and re-evaluating many of the traditional materials commonly used in tabla. I am examining the merit and purpose of them through my own philosophical perspective of music and life - to see if they serve a valid purpose, or not. Unfortunately, much of the used materials, be it in accompaniment or solo renditions, fail to convince me with a legitimate purpose. It also seems like the flaw may not be so much in the materials themselves, but in our failure to create relevance in the contemporary application of them.

Tabla's language is pretty abstract, not that easy to comprehend or relate to. It was not developed as a defined language of communication. The letters, words and phrases are more or less mimicry of the sounds produced from the drums. Those drum-notes, as I have felt, have the same capability of expression as their counterpart in the melodic notes – both equally abstract and ambiguous. There is an incredible amount of tonal possibility embedded in these drum-notes and the language thereof. So far, I haven't come across any sensible phonetic interpretation of these sounds and their related verbalizations. The most common practice has been to find some sort of similarity between the sounds of tabla and those from daily life or nature and make stories out of them. People rave about these stories. There are also sad instances of musicians resorting to meaningless display of skill-based gimmickry and circus. They serve only an immediate purpose, devoid of any greater value. The people, who use these gimmicks to gain fame, also get caught in their own trap forced to repeat them at every occasion to satisfy the expectation they create in their audience. To me it seems like a tragic consequence. I find nothing wrong in aspiring for fame and its package. But, trying to accomplish those through the pursuit of Indian classical music defies all rationale. It is similar to boarding a flight to Lhasa by mistake, instead of Las Vegas. Now, what to do? Trying to have a Las Vegas experience in Lhasa! That would be very unfortunate for both – the music and musician. It would bring down the quality of both.

Art is much more than skill. Skill may at best be only the means, not the end. To follow the evolutionary development of tabla's language and investigate into the hidden treasures of it cannot be done from a superficial level. It certainly calls for a much deeper delve.

I can see how the *Chilla* could easily become a dummy exercise for someone. It may easily turn into an absolutely brainless, thoughtless, feeling-less and robotic job. Perhaps that would be the more common experience out of looping the same materials over and over again, trying to chase a target. I find that extremely difficult to do. I always have great difficulty in doing something without involving my intellect and emotions to find a more defined purpose. May be I am a tad too serious. But, I do believe that intent always plays a major role in the ultimate quality of art. My mind would rarely allow me to do anything mechanically, without an artistic purpose. It can be a passive observer only for a while before it gets involved into the process.

There is yet another important issue I have. I don't want to chase a target; that's not what I am here for. What target is there for me to chase? Even if I pick up one, what will happen once I reach that target? Shall I look for another one and continue to look for more? Eventually, it may turn out that by chasing and reaching targets one after another I am only perpetuating my dissatisfaction and unhappiness. I would much rather save myself from this target exhaustion and conceive of this *Chilla* without nurturing any expectation of fruit. It may seem to be impossible to achieve, but that is what I am here to do - to devote myself fully, thoughtfully, philosophically and spiritually into this pursuit of music out of pure love for my simple, pure and sweet companion – the Tabla. That alone has been unimaginably the gratifying experience. I do battle with my inner self on several issues. But, those challenges only add more vitality to the flow.

It is true that I am using the timer, keeping practice and tempo charts. But, those are not my main driving force. They are like journals. We don't live a day to write a journal, the journal is merely a record of how we lived the day. The charts may also help in monitoring ourselves. Yet, to prevent them from becoming the motivational factor is easier said than done, even more so to someone conditioned by today's comparative and competitive mentality.

Day 32: August 11, 2016

Today is extremely hot and humid. Magdalena warned me about it in the morning. She turned both air-conditioners on and asked me to turn the fan on as needed. She worries about me even at work. Yesterday she heard me cough in the morning and kept worrying about me for the rest of the day until she found me okay in the evening. Such is her kindness.

I was forced to take two short naps. There was also a point when I was feeling suffocated. Perhaps there was too much of steam in the room. I opened the skylight windows for ventilation, it started feeling better. I could hear the birds around. I was wondering how the trees might be feeling under the unkind, scorching heat of the sun. The ones who give shade and shadow to others have no place to go under, when they need shelter.

It cooled off in the evening. Despite the heat, humidity and the consequent breaks, the practice today was slightly better than the last couple of days, both in terms of duration and quality. At about two hours past midnight the sky became clear to reveal the spectacular display of the Perseid Meteor shower.

Day 33: August 12, 2016

I was thinking about what I wrote on August 10th and was wondering where those thoughts came from. Do any of my peers worry about the present state of our music, or is it just me? Have I developed these observations because of living in New York for over two decades, exposed to a very high level of music and musical thoughts from all over the world? Does my academic background or my spiritual background have anything to do with these? I wonder, because apparently my fellow musicians seem to be just fine with the way things are. There is not much of a concern.

I was feeling bad about being so critical. Perhaps I shouldn't be. When it comes to feelings, I have no other choice but to be honest about them.

There is an element in our music, a calculated rhythmic ending pattern called the *tehai*. This application has been overemphasized in the last three decades or so. I have always wondered about the reason and philosophy behind it – what ultimate purpose does it serve? It almost seems like an IQ contest, which can never be part of my music. So, today I made a resolute decision to ignore the pressure of this modern trend and go on my way, free and confident.

My mind is filled with an uncertain kind of happiness. It is not happy about anything in particular, but about everything. It is a sense of contentedness, absorbed in the feeling that everything is just perfect and complete, it cannot be any better or any different from the way it is. It doesn't matter how long this feeling would last, there is no concern about that either.

In the middle of the day I decided to discard the practice chart. I detected that it was gradually taking over as a motivational factor and a wrong kind of motivation, for sure. I don't see the difference between practicing something for exactly two hours, or five minutes more or less than that. While choosing between dragging on something unmindfully and staying involved and focused, I would go for the second option as the more productive approach. I feel much better having the freedom to use or not use any kind of chart.

Day 34: August 13th, 2016

It rained all day today. There were continuous spells of heavy shower with lightning and thunder. In the afternoon Magdalena set me out under the patio umbrella, protected from the rain. Looking at the blue sky and green the fields all turn into grey and hazy, listening to all the different sounds of the rain coming down on different surfaces was an unparalleled experience. There was one lightning and thunder, the heaviest so far in my memory, which traveled across from one end to the other end of the sky, reminding of the meteor shower the other night. The sound of the thunder was reaching us a few seconds later. Bella had no argument with those thunders; she was absolutely quiet this time. Zorba was right by my leg, happily getting drenched. I have never seen such loyalty.

It is almost inexplicable how Zorba can be so different from Bella and many other dogs. He treats Bella as his sister. I have never seen Zorba making a sexual approach to Bella. When he plays with her, he doesn't fail to prove his seniority and superiority. But, also willfully surrenders to her in the fake fights to let her have the satisfaction of being the winner. In Magdalena's words "Bella is a thief, Zorba never steals." Anything he does, there is always a playful dignity in it. He is honest, loving, caring, loyal, self-restraint, diligent, intelligent and rational in his own way. He wasn't trained for any of these, this is his natural self. What would we call a person with such qualities?

The face of Zorba

Photo Credit: Josh Clemmons

The weather somehow took away some of the fire from my practice mentality. Tabla became wet in the morning. Magdalena turned on the air-conditioners to a setting where they would function more as dehumidifiers than coolers. I got back the fire of practice-passion later in the evening, which made it easy to go past midnight with real concentration. I don't know how long I practiced, because I have discarded the number calculations. Practicing purposefully as much and as long as possible with concentration and without causing damage to myself is the motto.

At some point today Magdalena had used the weighing scale in my bathroom as a door stopper. Trying to move it back to its position I had turned in on. Perhaps the motion did that. So, I climbed on it and found out that I am 182.2 pounds now, a 6.2 pounds decrease from July 10th.

Day 35: August 14th, 2016

Doing any work without the expectation of a result or reward seems almost impossible for mankind. Human beings are not programmed that way. And, in the process of growing up to deal with life, those elements of result and reward are further enforced onto our minds as the only motivational factors. How do you do away with those?

There has been a constant struggle within me to eliminate those motivational factors and practice just for the sake of practice. It is perhaps okay to specify areas of weaknesses to work on. But, in the process of working on them, it becomes extremely challenging to eliminate or even suspend the desire to get better at those.

Day 36: August 15th, 2016

This was a different day. The weather was playful with all aspects of light and shadow, heat and cool, dryness and humidity. My body and mind joined in the playfulness with lightness and freedom and got me fifteen hours of practice time. There were a few breaks for meals and bathroom. But, I took no nap. Actually, there was one point in the early afternoon when I dozed off a little in my seat.

It was the same process of analyzing the known materials, relearning some of them and developing them with touches of self-expression. Adding my own interpretation cannot be a mechanical process. I have to wait and wait until I am able to establish a communication with the piece. Some of the compositions can take a really long time. But, if something doesn't make sense today, doesn't mean that it never will. I shall have to wait till it does.

It was India's Independence Day. Several emotional and intellectual memories tend to pop up, asking for re-evaluation. Things are not as they seemed forty years ago.

I am still not sure what is in this number forty. Why did Christ, Mohammed and other leaders of the world choose this number for austerity? They must have had precedents before them to follow. I am not physically fasting, but there have been some austerities in this observance. It is quite interesting to notice that I had almost forgotten about my initial curiosity about this number forty. I don't know whether this signifies my indifference to the expectation of fruits.

Day 37: August 16th, 2016

A release from the known is needed to see the unknown. Space and Time seem to be the biggest contributors towards such release. Mind feels most comfortable within stored memories. Again and again it goes back to them to cling to, to fabricate on and to stay engaged in analysis and building up aspirations. To abandon such comfort needs a special practice of detachment. The starting point, in my experience, would be a sincere wish in finding a release from it.

Once that Wish-tree is planted, we need to keep nurturing and nourishing it. In course of our daily activities we may forget to do that. Or, even if we remember, we do it mechanically without much involvement. The tree is very sensitive in picking up our intentions. Detecting the decay in the genuineness of our interest and involvement, it may decide to wither away.

Life is very generous. It keeps on bringing us opportunities. So, in due course, we may plant another Wish-tree. Perhaps this time we will know better that maintaining is much harder than planting.

If and when the Tree grows, it will yield fruits of the unknown on its own.

Day 38: August 17th, 2016

As the full moon appeared on the evening sky, I found myself weeping. My fingers were engaged in playing a fast composition when this swell of emotion took over me. I was baffled to see myself in that uncontrollable condition. I asked myself "why are you crying"? It didn't answer; left me wondering.

Later at night, laying on my bed looking at the eyes of Zorba I found the answer. The full moon indicates that in a couple of days I shall be leaving this room. When I had entered this room it was just me. But now it is not just me, there is another presence in this room, which I shall be separating from. That presence, in its subtle form, has pervaded all of my being, offering me such immense joy and bliss of solitude.

How can we explain the nature of that presence?

Let me try in a round-about way. In some ritualistic practices, especially Hindu worships, they invoke and apply life to an inanimate object, like a sculpture or image. It is the first step to worship. With that application, the inanimate object becomes alive to be addressed and prayed to. At the end of the ceremony, the *lifetrone* in that object is deactivated and a symbolic immersion into water is performed.

In the pursuit of Indian music, musicians try to add life to the melodic and rhythmic modes called *Raga* and *Tala*, with an aspiration to perceive them as living entities. I don't know when and how my companion in this room came into existence. But, it has filled up so much of the space that I never had a sense of emptiness. Now what do I do? The thought of leaving that presence is breaking my heart. This is the hardest separation I have ever dealt with.

Day 39: August 18, 2016

The day was spent in pondering and wondering. Yesterday's pathos for separation has found reconciliation in the solace that nothing is going to be lost or left behind. The only things that can now be left behind are my past memories of such separation. I shall never again be separated from that presence. It is not a guest anymore; it is now a resident within me with its permanent seat. It will always be there for me ready to reappear whenever I am prepared to invoke and receive properly, irrespective of the time and space. I am overwhelmed with such generosity. Even though I don't know if I deserve it, perhaps I am better than what I think I am. This assurance came from within, from the same voice that has been guiding me all along.

Day 40: August 19, 2016

Is this truly the last day, end of the sacred path? If it is, shouldn't there be a feeling of exhaustion? Why am I not feeling anything like that at all? Instead, an inexhaustible freshness and vitality have permeated my entire being. It feels like only the beginning. Truly speaking, it is even better than how I felt forty days ago. How is that possible! I am feeling miraculously looser, lighter and free – both physically and mentally. This freedom is inexplicable, as if a bondage, which was around me for a long time, has fallen off. I feel ready for a new life, for a new emergence, for a new identity – to start all over again.

What am I going to do now with such renewed energy? What would be my objective from tomorrow? What would be the order of my priorities? How will I organize and maintain them? I feel an assurance from within that in the past forty days my mind already found and saved answers to all of these questions. It will reveal all in due course.

Life has always fascinated me with its splendors and charm. My senses are now more alert and awakened than before in perception, with readiness to zoom into the minutest details. There is so much more to see, hear, taste, smell, touch and feel. I am having goose bumps even thinking about the range of possibilities. My inquisitiveness has matured into fret-less childishness. I have more questions than answers. While one part of me was submerged and sedated in practice, the other part was churning the nectar.

It is time for me to –

Accept the invitation,

Dress up and be ready to join,

Embrace silence.

www.ingramcontent.com/pod-product-compliance
Lightning Source LLC
LaVergne TN
LVHW010306070426
835509LV00024B/3481